Kathleen Low, MLS

Legislative Reference Services and Sources

*Pre-publication
REVIEWS,
COMMENTARIES,
EVALUATIONS . . .*

"**L**egislative reference service is a form of special librarianship and, as such, often includes selective dissemination of information (SDI) and other current awareness services, document delivery, and extended reference and research. Low has written a very good survey, with insightful comments on promotion, marketing, and many other facets of operating a successful legislative information service. Low's warm and informal tone makes this book a pleasure to read. Public and academic librarians will find this book useful for collection development. Recommended for library schools and professionals serving clientele who need information on state legislative processes."

Library Journal

More pre-publication
REVIEWS, COMMENTARIES, EVALUATIONS . . .

"*L*egislative Reference Services and Sources is just what the 'doctor ordered'! Library services to legislators and staff have always been in need of a standard by which planning and training can be guided. This book puts services and sources together in a well-balanced set. The detailing of personalized professional services at a high level gives the legislative librarian a measurement to which services can be compared. The excellent justification for their services gives the working librarian a method and foundation for budgeting battles. Methods of gaining the trust and respect of legislative members are well explained with samples of letters, newsletters, bulletins, etc., provided.

Resources that are available to all levels of governmental users from city/county to state/federal are well defined and described. Special notes enable the 'new' legislative library staff member to recognize those most useful for their work. However, experienced legislative library members will find much to gain in their knowledge of such resources also."

Wynona M. Kimmel, MLS
Senior Librarian,
Chuckawalla Valley State Prison,
California

"*T*his specialized guide introduces librarians and researchers to a broad range of legislative reference sources. The resources are intended primarily to answer questions from lawmakers and legislators on complex issues relating to proposed legislation. However, grassroots organizers, new Americans seeking information on government agencies, students researching federal, state, and local governments, and in general, persons seeking information on elected officials, will find this guide a quick and easy resource directing them to appropriate sources to answer questions on broad and specific topics.

Librarians establishing a new service in the legislative arena will also find this a useful tool, not only for its resources, but also for the tips on how to actively promote and market the library's services, for dealing with issues of confidentiality and trust, and for providing after-hours access to the library.

In addition to the valuable information provided, the author's enthusiasm for providing good service and the fulfillment one receives in turn pervades the work and makes it a very worthwhile read."

Rhonda Rios Kravitz
Head of Access Services,
California State University
at Sacramento

"**A**ll fine reference works rely on certain basic characteristics to determine their worth. They are praised or condemned based on the clarity and conciseness of their organization, the correctness of their entries, and their usefulness. *Legislative Reference Services and Sources* is a concise, clearly written, well-organized reference work that contains all of the information and cited sources necessary to set up and successfully manage a legislative library.

The section on core resources pays for the entire book. It consists of an in-depth annotated list of legislative resources that includes everything from dictionaries and directories to the various 'online databases and systems particularly useful in legislative reference.' Its usefulness as a comprehensive buying guide is not only for legislative librarians but for any library with a need for this type of material, from small governmental agency libraries to the most well-equipped state or academic library. The annotations are concise and thorough in touching on the most salient aspect of each title listed. The information on online databases and systems is just enough to make an informed decision on whether to contact a particular vendor.

This work is a veritable model for establishing, managing, and marketing legislative reference services. It can be used by any type of library in its entirety or only certain sections used to meet individual needs. It is recommended for all types of libraries whether special or for a more general clientele."

Audrey Dodds Moore, MLS
Reference Services Manager,
California State Library,
Sacramento

More pre-publication
REVIEWS, COMMENTARIES, EVALUATIONS . . .

"**A**t last! a 'bible' for legislative reference librarians.

This publication is a tremendous accomplishment for one person to have assembled. Nothing this complete has ever been published. Committees have compiled lists of references and publications, but this is the most complete text ever published. The book will be welcomed by all legislative reference librarians: those with experience, and most especially those new to the field.

It would be difficult to select any section as most valuable, since all sections are excellent. If any portion stands out, it would be the one on online reference, since the provision of this service for the legislature is unique, and the author's expertise and experience in this area is outstanding.

This publication will be helpful not only to legislative librarians, but to many other types of libraries which provide reference to a specialized clientele."

Irene V. Stone
Supervising Librarian (Retired),
California State Library

"**K**athleen Low has written a most welcome overview of the various ways library information services may be structured within government or special libraries. The material is clearly presented by a Principal Librarian with comprehensive on-the-ground experience and knowledge of the foibles of her legislative clientele. The work takes a practical how-to-do-it approach with a logical layout evidenced in the detailed table of contents. Of particular benefit is the review of hard copy and online reference resources and explication of their value and limitations. I enjoyed the specificity of the appendices with their copyable examples."

Lucy A. Martin
Library Technical Assistant (Retired),
State Information
and Reference Service,
California State Library

The Haworth Press, Inc.

Legislative Reference
Services and Sources

HAWORTH Library and Information Science
Peter Gellatly, Editor in Chief

New, Recent, and Forthcoming Titles:

The In-House Option: Professional Issues of Library Automation by T. D. Webb

British University Libraries by Toby Burrows

Women Online: Perspectives on Women's Studies in Online Databases edited by Steven D. Atkinson and Judith Hudson

Buyers and Borrowers: The Application of Consumer Theory to the Study of Library Use by Charles D. Emery

Broadway's Prize-Winning Musicals: An Annotated Guide for Libraries and Audio Collectors by Leo N. Miletich

Academic Libraries in Greece: The Present Situation and Future Prospects edited by Dean H. Keller

Introductory CD ROM Searching: The Key to Effective Ondisc Searching by Joseph Meloche

Legislative Reference Services and Sources by Kathleen Low

Legislative Reference Services and Sources

Kathleen Low, MLS

The Haworth Press
New York • London • Norwood (Australia)

The Haworth Press, Inc., 10 Alice Street, Binghamton, NY 13904-1580

Library of Congress Cataloging-in-Publication Data

Low, Kathleen.
    Legislative reference services and sources / by Kathleen Low.
       p.   cm.
    Includes bibliographical references and index.
    ISBN 1-56024-891-2 (alk. paper)
    1. Legislative reference bureaus–United States–States.   2. Government libraries–United States–States. 3. Government information–United States–States.
JK2497.L98   1994
027.6'5–dc20
                                                93-39408
                                                 CIP

Dedicated with love to
Harry, Rose, Susan, and Carrie

ABOUT THE AUTHOR

Kathleen Low, MLS, is a Principal Librarian at the California State Library. Previously, as Outreach Services Manager, she managed the library's Capitol Branch which provides reference services to the state legislature. She has also been Coordinator of Online Services for the Cooperative Library Agency for Systems and Services (CLASS). Ms. Low has written a number of articles for *The Reference Librarian, American Libraries, Library Hi-Tech News,* and other professional publications and has spoken at various meetings and conferences. She is a member of the Librarians Division of the National Conference of State Legislatures, the American Library Association, the Northern California Technical Processes Group, and the Association of State Writers and Editors.

CONTENTS

Preface

Legislative reference bureaus are similar to special libraries in that they serve a particular clientele with specific needs that must be met. But they differ from special libraries in that they do not deal with a specific discipline, but rather with a full spectrum of subject areas. And they can often be organizations unto themselves.

The men and women who are hired to work in a legislative reference bureau will find the work intriguing and enlightening. Unfortunately, something they will not find are current texts focusing on legislative reference services to provide them with an introduction to the world of legislative reference. This book helps to fill that void. In it the reader is provided with an overview of legislative reference services and is acquainted with over 100 sources useful in responding to information requests from legislators and other lawmakers.

This book grew out of my own need for such information. Many years ago when I was hired to manage a branch of a state library that provided reference services to the legislature and executive office, I desperately searched for texts that could assist me in my new task only to find no current texts existed. I relied heavily and gratefully on other professionals in the field.

I want to express my sincere thanks to Irene Stone, who taught me what I needed to know to manage a legislative reference service and who was always happy to assist me when I sought her advice. Her ongoing encouragement of my professional endeavors led me to undertake this project. I also want to express my sincere thanks to Audrey Dobbs Moore of the California State Library, whose support and assistance I could always rely upon.

Chapter 1

Introduction

Reference services play a vital role in the legislative process. The information provided by a legislative reference service (LRS) enables legislators and their staff to thoroughly examine complex issues as they arise. Their action on an issue will be based upon their knowledge of it. The more knowledgeable they are of the issue, the better able they will be to deal with it.

Legislative reference services (LRS), or reference bureaus as they are also known, serve several functions. The first and foremost is to provide legislators and their staff with the information they need to effectively perform their duties. Providing this information entails actively acquiring relevant materials and organizing them so that they can be easily retrieved. In addition to books and periodicals, most legislative reference services also collect and maintain files of other materials such as newspaper clippings of selected topics, press releases from the offices of executive officers, state road maps, etc. Easy access to the information contained in these materials is provided by LRS staff to both onsite and offsite patrons.

A second function of the LRS is to facilitate access to the actual materials in the library's collection. LRS staff identify, retrieve, and forward library materials to patrons in response to requests for information on broad or specific topics. LRS staff act as deliverers rather than gatekeepers of the information.

The third function of a LRS is to secure materials from other services as needed by its clients. This encompasses borrowing materials from other libraries or purchasing materials for or on behalf of patrons who may wish to keep their interest in a specific item or topic confidential. Documents are also ordered through document delivery services as needed.

The fourth function of a legislative reference service is to alert its clientele to new materials of potential interest to them. This is usually accomplished by issuing lists of new acquisitions, making available a selective dissemination of information service, or compiling and distributing of bibliographies or lists of new acquisitions on topics of government interest. In situations where the technology exists, legislators can be alerted to the availability of new materials through electronic mail or internal electronic bulletin boards.

The role of the librarian or information professional is to perform any tasks necessary to support the functions of the legislative reference service. This includes creating an environment receptive to requests for information and encouraging use of the LRS through various promotional activities. The librarian is also responsible for making the service accessible through various mediums, such as telephone, electronic mail, etc. The librarian is the primary contact between the LRS and its patrons, requiring the librarian to efficiently ascertain the information needed by its clientele. It is the librarian who can instill patron confidence in the LRS by maintaining the confidentiality of requests and providing accurate, complete responses to requests in a timely manner.

On a daily basis the librarian must purchase or acquire materials that will fulfill the anticipated needs of its clientele. These materials should include legislative publications such as bills and legislative histories, and all of these materials should be organized and housed in a facility easily accessible to the service's clientele.

The librarian must be familiar with other libraries and information resources both in and outside of the area. Special and academic libraries, various government agencies, trade and professional associations, and key individuals are a sample of other information resources that may be tapped for information or materials. Knowledge of these resources enables the librarian to offer an effective interlibrary borrowing and reference service. The function of the librarian is to keep the legislative reference service functioning properly, efficiently, and effectively. The librarian can create either a positive or negative impression of the service, and keep the services of the LRS in the minds of its patrons.

Probably one of the best ways to get an overview of the functions of an LRS and its staff is to take a look at what occurs on a daily basis. On a typical day the legislative reference bureau receives numerous requests primarily over the telephone or from walk-in patrons. These requests generally differ from those received in a public or academic library in the topics, the way in which the information will be used, and the extent of services provided by LRS staff in response to these requests. For instance, the following requests may be received in an hour. A legislative staff person calls in a request for how a specific legislator voted on 13 specific bills from the past session and needs the information by the end of the day. A senator calls from the floor of the Senate while the legislature is in session and needs to know the current number of prisoners incarcerated in the state. He or she will stay on the line while you find the answer. Another legislator calls to request comprehensive information on disposable diapers and solid waste composting, including which states have the service available, details on the actual process, and the actual annual volume of disposable diapers composted in each of the states where the service is available. A patron walks in requesting a list of those states that have laws pertaining to the release of personal motor vehicle registration information to the public upon request and would like a copy of the actual laws sent to his office by the end of the week. Meanwhile, a written request is received from an executive officer who needs to know where the state ranks both nationally and internationally in terms of educational quality, the amount of dollars spent per student at the high school level, the amount of dollars spent annually to lure high technology businesses to the state, and the number of industry/state college partnerships currently in existence. The legislative librarian will respond to all of these requests and provide the patrons with the information sought.

The ultimate goal of the LRS is to supply legislators and their staff with the information they need to effectively examine, draft, or enact legislation of benefit to the public. To fulfill this goal, the LRS staff must respond to all requests received from legislators and their staff in a nonpartisan manner, providing the most complete and accurate responses to their requests. The LRS staff must be professionals dedicated to providing quality service.

The location of the legislative reference service in the organizational structure of government varies considerably at the state level.

The unit may be under a partisan legislative committee, or under a nonpartisan office (such as the Legislative Analyst's Office), or each house of the legislature may maintain its own reference bureau. In many instances the LRS may be part of a government agency, such as the state library.

Where the LRS resides within the government structure influences what services it may provide and to whom these are provided. If the unit resides under a partisan office of the legislature, the LRS would generally only provide services to a selected group of users. If the LRS resides under a nonpartisan legislative unit, such as the Legislative Counsel's office, it would probably serve all members of the legislature and executive offices and may also provide a variety of other services such as bill drafting or bill analysis. Whereas, if the LRS is part of a nonlegislative unit such as a state library, it may provide reference services to all who may be interested.

Whether the LRS serves only legislative staff or the public at large, the LRS staff is responsible for providing patrons with the data they need to facilitate the legislative process. Meeting the needs of users can be stressful at times, but the reference staff members who successfully meet those information needs will find the work very self-rewarding.

All too often reference librarians lack the opportunity to see the end result of the information they provide. Legislative librarians are fortunate in being able to frequently see the results of their labors. Much of the information they provide to legislative staff is used to draft legislation, and they will commonly find legislators for whom they have supplied information introducing a bill on that topic in the very near future. Nothing can be more satisfying on a daily basis than knowing that as a legislative librarian, your work is helping shape the society in which you live.

Chapter 2

Origin of Legislative Reference Services

The exact origins of legislative reference services is unclear; scholars disagree as to who originated the service and where it first began. Some attribute its origin to Melvil Dewey. Known as an innovator, when he took charge as State Librarian at the New York State Library in 1890 he was credited for establishing a Division of Sociology, the functions of which included gathering pertinent materials for legislators and preparing an index of current legislation. The Division, under the direct charge of Dr. R.H. Whitten, later evolved into the Legislative Reference Section.

Other scholars credit Charles McCarthy for the innovative origin of legislative reference. In 1901 the State of Wisconsin authorized the Free Library Commission to establish and maintain a library for use by state legislators. Dr. McCarthy was charged with the task. He envisioned the services of the Legislative Reference Department as providing legislators with sound and accurate information and advice in as rapid a fashion as needed to draft legislation. To this extent, he expanded services to include collecting all ranges of materials that may be needed by legislators. He also went so far as to occasionally evaluate legislation. He believed his service should provide whatever assistance required by his patrons, regardless of its importance or relevance to the legislative process. He also took on a role of actively acquainting himself with his patrons, seeking out their information needs, and promoting the use of the library's services. His work did not go unnoticed by librarians across the nation from the federal to municipal level.

At the municipal level, Baltimore, in 1907, was the first city to establish a legislative reference service. Designated as the Baltimore Department of Legislative Reference, the department's purpose was to collect, compile, and index information on topics of potential interest to the mayor and municipal officials. In the succeeding years, legislative reference services began appearing in a number of major cities ranging from Cleveland to St. Louis.

The "movement" started by Charles McCarthy did not go unnoticed at the federal level either. Beginning in 1907, several members of Congress, including Wisconsin's Senator LaFollette and Representative John Nelson, introduced bills to establish a legislative reference service despite the fact that the Library of Congress had been providing many services offered by legislative reference bureaus like that in Wisconsin. Nonetheless, in 1906 Congress appropriated $25,000 to enable the Librarian of Congress, Herbert Putnam, to hire staff to prepare an index to the Statutes at Large, digests, and compilations of law as requested by Congress. However, this did not happen until 1914, when an amendment to the legislative, executive, and judicial appropriation included a line item for legislative reference. That amendment is regarded as the first official establishment and recognition of the Library of Congress' legislative reference services.

Chapter 3

Basic Legislative Reference Services

Providing reference services to legislative and public officials can be very demanding and rewarding at the same time. Your patrons demand the maximum level of services, with a complete response expected within their time frames, regardless of how short a period that time frame may be. The information they request from you is an integral part of the overall data they need to meet their own deadlines. In effect, they are putting their trust in you to deliver accurate information to them in a timely fashion.

At times meeting these expectations can be difficult and stressful. Your ability to successfully respond to their requests will, however, bring you a deep sense of accomplishment and a feeling of having made a significant contribution to society. On a regular basis you will gather information on various aspects in a range of topics as requested. And with the same frequency you will become aware of the introduction of new bills on topics for which you gathered the initial background information, thus having the opportunity to see the role you played in the legislative process.

This chapter provides an overview of the services needed by legislative officials. Their needs often extend beyond those met by services commonly provided by public and academic libraries. On a daily basis these patrons must respond to constituent requests, they must draft or evaluate proposed legislation, and they must stay abreast of events and issues from the local to the national level.

To meet their needs, you must be prepared to respond to requests pertaining to a wide array of disciplines. You must stay abreast of current events in anticipation of relevant requests, and you must be prepared to provide your patrons with the maximum level of service you can provide. This often means crossing the line from reference into research. And there is no taboo in crossing this line as long as you have defined the level of services to be provided to your patrons.

The services provided by legislative reference libraries or bureaus in the states range from reference services to major research. Other services provided by the libraries may include bill drafting, distribution of legislative publications, and legal counseling. We will focus on those services most commonly provided to legislative officials.

READY REFERENCE

Provision of ready reference services is an integral part of your overall services–it is a part valued by your patrons. Because of the time pressures they face, rapid fulfillment of their requests is essential to providing good service. Frequently ready reference information is requested minutes before it is needed for a press conference, floor session, or similar impending event.

Many of the ready reference requests will pertain to legislative and legal matters, such as the final status or sponsor of specific bills from previous sessions. Patrons may request the full citations and decision of recent court cases, the telephone number of court clerks, or the chapter or public law number of a bill signed into law. Other ready reference requests frequently include the correct wording or author of a quote, the full text or portions of a speech recently made by a public official, statistical facts, as well as forms of international protocol. Although the topics of the ready reference requests may be different from what you are familiar with, the process of locating the answers to these requests is the same as any other reference request.

SUBJECT REFERENCE AND RESEARCH

Legislators are in constant need of information on numerous topics as they try to address diverse issues of public concern. The depth of information they need on a specific topic can range from a one- or two-paragraph overview of a subject as needed to respond to a letter from a constituent, to comprehensive information on an issue or problem to be addressed by proposed legislation. The type of information desired is commonly textual or statistical, and to a lesser extent visual.

Each patron expects a specific response to his or her subject request. Some will expect you to locate and provide them with the specific text which will answer a question they may have. Others anticipate receiving various materials that may contain the specific data they are seeking, while others may only desire to be directed to potential sources of information because they prefer to do their own reference or research.

Their subject requests can take many forms. For instance, a patron may ask for a list of all studies done in the last 15 years on chinook salmon in the upper Sacramento River. Meanwhile another patron may request a survey and citation list of indecency laws in the 50 states. And yet another patron may want news articles pertaining to a recent medical discovery.

Many of your clients' requests will cross the boundary from reference into research. This boundary is irrelevant to them and should remain so. It is up to you and/or your supervisors to decide which requests necessitate actual research, and whether or not you can provide them with the information or answers they need. Subject reference assistance is a service provided by almost every library dealing with public officials. The level of this assistance varies, and often will extend into research services.

INFORMATION VERIFICATION

Issuing correct verifiable facts and information to the public is fundamental to the credibility of public officials. On a regular basis you will receive requests to verify data such as bibliographic citations, the correct spelling of personal names, or dates of upcoming events. You will also be called upon to verify other types of information that can be categorized as statistical, biographical, or event based. Two of these types of information often prove to be the most elusive to verify.

Because statistics can be presented in various ways to make them effective, they can be hard to verify in the exact form in which they are submitted to you. For example, you may be asked to verify the statement that "four out of every nine people in the state lack health insurance.'' Immediate problems with this statement include the lack of a date or time frame in which the statement was made, the lack of a date of reference in which the statistic is drawn (i.e., does it reflect data from two years ago or last month?), and lack of any indication as to who is included in the statistical count (residents as well as non-residents, children and adults, Medi-Cal recipients). With this minimal level of information you could spend hours trying to locate and reconcile various statistics to verify the statement. With access to full-text online databases you may find the statement has appeared in a news article that hopefully quotes the source. Otherwise, be prepared to devote adequate time to verify the data as thoroughly as possible. Also, do not hesitate to inform your patrons of the difficulty of verifying certain statements, and what they may expect, and when.

Another type of information commonly difficult to verify is certain pieces of biographical data. An individual who prefers to keep his or her personal life private is usually successful in doing so unless the individual basques in celebrity status. So efforts to find and verify other than basic biographical data (i.e., date of birth, etc.) on low profile scholars, officials, and others may prove fruitless at times.

Somewhat easier to verify are events such as traffic accidents, fires, riots, natural disasters, or scientific or medical discoveries. This category also includes such events as embarrassing or controversial remarks made by public officials. Usually all of these events are well covered in the media, or are reported as part of an official record.

Because some requests to verify data take only minutes while others may take hours or days, you should have a policy or guidelines in place as to the extent of time that staff will work on a given request. These guidelines will give staff a gauge for measuring what can be considered a reasonable amount of time to spend on any given request, and also what can be considered satisfactory service in responding to these requests.

ASSISTANCE WITH CONSTITUENT QUESTIONS

The level of service provided to legislative members or staff in relation to constituent requests varies as vastly from library to library as the actual requests. The only typical characteristic of constituent requests is that they are atypical! The requests can be appeals for assistance to disprove commonly accepted theories or facts or basic information about the legislative process from a child's school assignment. Other requests may be for help in locating specific information, or compilation of historical or statistical state data. Some libraries will provide a minimum level of services in these instances, simply by referring the patron to potential sources of the information, whereas other libraries will provide the actual information needed to respond to the request. The Wisconsin Legislative Reference Bureau takes the service even one step further. When requested, they will answer constituent requests on a legislator's behalf.

Regardless of the level of service your library decides to provide for these questions, it is important that your patrons know what that level is. If only minimal service is provided for these requests, your patrons need to know that this is not the overall level of service provided for all requests, but simply for these *specific* requests. Your patrons need not only to differentiate these constituent requests from other requests in their mind, but they also need to inform you at the time they submit their request what type of request it is so that you can provide the appropriate level of service.

SDI AND CURRENT AWARENESS SERVICES

SDI (selective dissemination of information) and current awareness services keep your clients abreast of new publications in their field of interest. This is accomplished by issuing bibliographies of new materials on selected topics of particular, current, or emerging interest on a periodic basis. The SDI services offered by commercial information services such as DIALOG Information Services and Mead Data Central's LEXIS/NEXIS system simplify gathering and printing the citations and data needed to produce these publications.

Before initiating a current awareness service you need to assess the areas of interest and the information needs of your patrons at large, or individually for an SDI request. This is an ongoing process that should be completed at least once a year, preferably every quarter. You should also encourage your patrons to contact you with suggestions for current awareness publications.

The current awareness services of most libraries consist of the preparation and distribution of brief reports and/or bibliographies on topics of interest at the appropriate level of government in which you are employed. Issues such as term limits affect all levels of government, but the publications prepared by your reference service should reflect materials on the topic as it relates to your target audience. For example, a bibliography of new materials on term limits issued by a state library would focus primarily on the topic as it may affect state government, whereas a county library's publications would target its application to county government. Since you respond to requests for information from your patrons on a daily basis, you are in the best position to spot topics of emerging interest. Preparation of current awareness materials on these topics will ultimately save you the time of having to repeatedly gather the same information for different patrons.

SDI, or a selective dissemination of information services, differs from current awareness services in that SDI services are targeted toward individual users, where current awareness services are aimed at a wider audience. In an SDI service, new literature is scanned on a regular basis and bibliographies on specific topics are compiled at the request of individual patrons. However, depending upon the topic, the bibliography may be of interest to other users. For example, if the ongoing topic of a specific SDI request is prenatal care, members of the health committee or individuals in the appropriate department of health services may also be interested in receiving a copy of a list of new publications addressing the topic. Do not be shy. Forward a sample copy of the list or bibliography to others who may be dealing with the topic and ask them if they would be interested in receiving future lists on the topic. This allows the information prepared for an SDI request to be used by more than one individual.

DOCUMENT DELIVERY

Supplying patrons with the actual materials that fulfill their information needs is the final step in completion of a request. Supplying the materials is often interpreted as simply setting aside the appropriate materials for the patron to review or take away with them. This is fine if your patrons are accustomed to stopping by the library. In actuality, however, a number of your patrons may never visit the library. Their requests are submitted over the telephone or by written request, and they subsequently ask that the information or materials be delivered, sent, or transmitted via facsimile machine to their offices. Delivering materials to your patrons' offices as needed can be construed as providing them with the maximum level of service in document delivery.

The importance of timely delivery of materials to patrons depends partly upon the proximity of the library to the majority of your patrons. If the majority of your patrons work at an inconvenient distance from your facility, you should consider establishing a regular delivery service to their office, or a delivery point or satellite service in their building where they can pick up materials. By doing so, you are ensuring that your patrons have easy access to the information and materials requested.

Several libraries make use of an offsite materials delivery point where library materials may be picked up or returned. The New York State Library, for example, maintains several service points for their patrons where they can pick up and return materials. Other services are also provided at these service points. The California State Library also maintains a service point in the state capitol building where patrons can pick up and return materials as well as submit requests. Materials requested by patrons are delivered to the capitol site twice a day.

If many of your patrons do work at distant locations, you will undoubtedly be asked to transmit information to their offices via facsimile machine. This is a convenient method of delivery for certain types of information such as photocopies of pages from books or journals. If your computer is equipped with a facsimile modem, you also have the capability of downloading online database search results to disk, then sending them to your patrons through use of your facsimile modem. Although for some materials, such as poor copies of newspaper articles, the quality of the print is not always satisfactory to the patron. Nonetheless, transmission of information via facsimile machines is a fast method of delivering information to your clients. You should have a written guideline or policy in place regarding what information will or will not be sent via facsimile machine to patrons' offices, and when (i.e., on demand, as staff time permits, etc.) it will be sent.

Another component of document delivery not to be forgotten is the library's ability to obtain materials from other libraries for your patrons. The interlibrary loan service provides your patrons with materials otherwise inaccessible to them. The ILL function enables you to better serve them.

BILL TRACKING, LEGISLATIVE HISTORIES,
AND OTHER SERVICES

Legislative reference libraries and bureaus often provide a variety of other services to their clients depending upon how the unit is organized, and its purpose. In some states the reference bureau is charged with drafting bills. For example, the Wisconsin statutes require the Wisconsin Legislative Reference Bureau to draft all bills, joint resolutions, and simple amendments introduced in the legislature, as well as prepare analyses of the bills. Attorneys are employed by the Wisconsin Legislative Reference Bureau to perform these tasks.

Another service provided by some reference services includes researching the history of specific pieces of legislation. These legislative histories can include the voting record of legislators on the bill, and the legislation's intent. This service can consume considerable staff time.

Some reference bureaus also prepare publications or documents of legislative interest. These documents may be indexes to legislative journals or lists of past hearings and resulting reports. Compilation of a guide to government that provides an overview and key facts is another type of publication some reference bureaus prepare for their respective legislatures or governing body.

The services provided by legislative reference bureaus vary depending upon the needs of their users. Flexibility and responsiveness to the changing needs of the user are indispensable.

Chapter 4

Core Resources

Supporting every legislative reference service is a working collection of resource materials relied upon by staff and patrons. The collection consists of handbooks, manuals, directories, legal materials, journals, and other materials that provide them with pertinent information on a daily basis. This chapter will present materials that are frequently found in legislative library collections. The items cited are either targeted at legislative users, or are devoted to, or contain information of legislative interest. Other commonly used materials with a general focus, such as the *Encyclopedia of Associations* and the *World Almanac* are not included.

Many of the resources librarians rely upon are not restricted to a print format. So information on pertinent online resources and associations have also been included in this chapter.

PRINTED RESOURCES

Dictionaries frequently define directories as simply "books listing the names, addresses, etc., of a specific group of persons." But in reality, they are the key to people who possess information you or your patron may be seeking. Directories of legislative policy specialists, librarians, and leaders identify resource people in a given subject or occupation who possess or have accessible specific data by nature of their position or office. The fastest or possibly the only way to retrieve information you may be seeking is through contact with a specific resource person.

Directories can also provide information on the structure of an organization by nature of the hierarchy of entries within an agency or government. A good example are federal government directories, which list information for the parent department, with entries for subordinate offices appearing below the parent department.

Congressional and Federal Directories

Congressional Staff Directory (Staff Directories Ltd., Mt. Vernon, VA) Semiannual.

This directory provides useful brief biographical information on congressional staff as well as the members of Congress. Since initial and regular contacts regarding bills and legislative programs is usually through a congressional staff employee, rather than the member, the directory provides valuable background information on key staff people you or your patrons may be dealing with on a regular basis. Both a personal name and subject index are included.

Congressional Yellow Book (Monitor Publishing Co., Washington, DC) Quarterly.

Subtitled "Who's Who in Congress, Including Committees and Key Staff," the book contains photographs, brief biographical data, committee assignments, and key staff aids of all U.S. Congressional Members. Other features of this publication are state delegation and district maps, a list of zip codes by congressional district, and a congressional staff index.

Federal Executive Directory (Carroll Publishing Co., Washington, DC) 6 issues per year.

This directory covers executives in the Executive Office of the President, Cabinet level departments, administrative agencies, and Congressional Offices. The entries for the congressional members include a brief biographical profile and listings for key staff. Directory information for House and Senate Committees, and other congressional offices is likewise available. A keyword index facilitates access to the information.

Federal Regional Executive Directory (Carroll Publishing Co., Washington, DC) Semiannual.

Identifying and locating the telephone numbers and addresses of key federal personnel in regional office is easy with access to this directory. In addition to federal regional offices, it lists key personnel of federal courts, contacts for military installations, and the state offices of U.S. Congresspersons. Keyword and geographic indexes appear at the end of the directory.

Federal Regulatory Directory (Congressional Quarterly Inc., Washington, DC) Quadrennial.

This directory contains profiles of federal regulatory agencies, which includes a brief history and organization of the agency, its regulatory powers, key people within the agency, and their addresses and telephone numbers. The profiles also include contacts for additional sources of information.

Federal Staff Directory (Staff Directories Ltd., Mt. Vernon, VA) Annual.

This directory lists the names, addresses, and phone numbers of key people in the federal bureaucracy. It includes over 2600 brief federal executive biographies and is organized into four main categories. The first category, the Executive Office of the President, encompasses not only White House offices and the Office of the Vice President, but agencies of the Executive Office and Presidential Advisory Organizations as well. The second section focuses on executive departments from the Department of Agriculture to the Department of Veterans Affairs. Section three includes the independent agencies such as the Advisory Commission on Intergovernmental Relations and the Office of Government Ethics. The final section, "Quasi-Official, International, and Non-Government Organizations" includes those entities that do not fit in any of the previous categories or agencies that are private, government chartered. Examples of these entities include the Federal Home Loan Mortgage Corporation, the John F. Kennedy Center for the Performing Arts, AMTRAK, etc. A personal name index and keyword in context subject index are included.

Federal Yellow Book (Monitor Publishing Co., Washington, DC) Quarterly.

Directory information on federal departments and independent federal agencies and the Office of the President and Vice President can be found in this publication. One nice feature of this directory is that it contains a section devoted to regional offices.

Taylor's Encyclopedia of Government Officials: Federal and State (Political Research Inc., Dallas, TX) Biennial.

One of the major attractions of this directory is its illustrations. It contains maps, photographs of legislators, and in many instances, even a photograph of the state's capitol building, and a picture of the state seal. Published after each general election, the directory contains state legislative officials, federal legislative and executive leaders, and justices of the U.S. Supreme Court.

Washington Representatives (Columbia Books Inc., Washington, DC) Annual.

The coverage of this Washington D.C. directory is different from most in that its primary focus is not on federal congressional personnel. Although it does include federal legislative personnel, its primary focus is on lobbyists, representatives of national associations, labor unions, special interest groups, registered foreign agents, major corporations, and other key people in Washington who play a role in shaping federal legislation. A subject index and foreign interest index are contained in the directory.

Who's Who in American Politics (R.R. Bowker, New Providence, NJ) Biennial.

A biographical directory, it contains entries for over 25,000 politicians from the federal to state level. These politicians include mayors of cities with populations over 50,000, state elected officials, supreme court justices, members of the U.S. Congress, federal executive officers, and political party chairs. The entries are arranged by state, then alphabetically by biographee. A personal name index is included.

State Directories

Directory of Governors of the American States, Commonwealth and Territories (National Governors' Association, Washington, DC) Semiannual.

This directory contains photographs and brief biographical information on state governors in the U.S., Puerto Rico, and American Protectorates. It also contains information on their terms of office and key staff people.

Directory of Legislative Leaders (National Conference of State Legislatures, Denver, CO) Annual.

A nice quick reference guide, this directory lists full contact information for state legislative leaders across the United States, including all presiding majority and minority leaders, with their preferred capitol and district addresses and phone numbers. Also listed are the legislators' staff director or other key staff members, including their appointment secretaries.

50-State Legislative Directory (California Journal Press, Sacramento, CA) Annual, looseleaf.

For each of the states it includes the names, addresses, districts, and party affiliation of each state legislator and Congressional Member. The publication also includes a section on committees, which lists the members of various state legislative committees plus their political party affiliations.

Legislative Librarians Directory (National Conference of State Legislatures, Denver, CO) Annual.

For each state, the directory lists full contact information for legislative research librarians, as well as those for American protectorates and Canada.

State Administrative Officials Classified by Function (Council of State Governments, Lexington, KY) Biennial.

This valuable reference directory lists contact information for thousands of state officials in specific areas of government ranging from corporate records to state-local relations. The entries in this directory are grouped by functional category, such as public welfare, social services, alcoholic beverage control, etc., then listed alphabetically by state.

State Elective Officials and the Legislatures (Council of State Governments, Lexington, KY) Biennial.

This directory includes the names and addresses of elected state executive officials, state legislators, and state court of last resort judges. Arranged by state, the book contains about two to three pages devoted to each state. The prefatory material includes a U.S. map of political party control by governorship, by state legislature in the Senate, and by state legislature in the House or Assembly. Also included is a summary table of the number of legislators in each state, their party affiliation, and term of office.

State Executive Directory (Carroll Publishing Co., Washington, DC) Published three times per year.

The first section of this directory, "Organizational Listing of

State Governments," includes the names, titles, addresses, and phone numbers of executive officials in all 50 states and Puerto Rico and other territories. The second section lists legislative officials. Listings of state Supreme Courts, state offices in Washington, DC, legislative sessions, governors, and state capitols are also included.

State Legislative Leadership Committees and Staff (Council of State Governments, Lexington, KY) Biennial.

Divided by state, the directory lists the names, addresses, and phone numbers of legislative officers and principal staff. It also lists the names and chairpersons of standing legislative committees, plus legislative agencies that serve the legislature. The second portion of this work contains directory information for selected legislative committees, and selected officers.

State Yellow Book (Monitor Publishing Co., Washington, DC) Semiannual.

For each of the states this book provides directory information on public officials in the executive and legislative branches. One section is devoted to profiles of each state that includes data on its government structure, history, demography, geography, economy, and other information. A subject index and name index are included at the back of the directory.

Local and Municipal Directories

County Executive Directory (Carroll Publishing Co., Washington, DC) Semiannual.

The names, addresses, and phone numbers of county administrators, council members, board of supervisors, and other county executives in the U.S. can be located in this directory. The entries are listed alphabetically by state and are grouped in one of two sections, those with populations over 25,000 and those with populations under 25,000.

Directory of City Policy Officials (National League of Cities, Washington, DC) Annual.

Within this publication you will find the names, addresses, and telephone numbers of the chief elected officials and administrative officers in the cities and municipalities with populations over

30,000. A bonus piece of information contained in the directory is the expiration dates of terms for the various elected officials.

Municipal Executive Directory (Carroll Publishing Co., Washington, DC) Semiannual.

The names, addresses, and telephone numbers of mayors, city managers, and other municipal executives for over 7,000 cities, towns, and villages are included in this publication. For municipalities with populations over 15,000, the directory includes its population and county as well. The names and addresses of council members are also provided for municipalities with populations over 25,000. A geographic index is contained at the end of the publication.

Other Directories

Directory of Political Periodicals (Government Research Service, Topeka, KS) Annual (ISSN 1057-0578).

Journals, newsletters, and newspapers focusing on U.S. government and politics are listed in this publication; however, academic political science journals are excluded. The entry for each title listed includes the publisher, address, telephone number, editor, price, frequency, whether or not advertising is accepted, and other information such as the publication's size, ISSN, etc. The directory includes a subject index with titles focusing on a particular state.

Handbooks, Manuals, and Almanacs

The handbooks, manuals, and almanacs cited in this section were selected because they are either targeted for use by legislative staff or are heavily consulted by them. Again, commonly consulted works of a broad topical nature, such as the *U.S. Statistical Abstract*, are not presented here.

Almanac of American Politics (National Journal, Washington, DC) Biennial.

Within this almanac readers will find analytical profiles of the members of the U.S. Congress and the governors of all 50 states. The information on each individual profile includes brief biographical and career information, lobby group ratings, National Journal ratings, and key votes. An overview of the characteristics of each congressional district is also included. This publication is very similar to *Politics in America.*

Almanac of the Fifty States (Information Publications, Palo Alto, CA) Annual.

This almanac provides statistical and comparative ranking data for the states. In the first part of the almanac, "State Profiles," the book presents an approximate eight-page profile of each state containing data on its geography and environment, demographics and population, vital statistics and health, education, welfare and social programs, housing, government finance, government elections, crime and law enforcement, labor and income, business and industry, and communication, energy, and transportation.

The second part of the book contains tables of the ranking of the states according to various factors such as population, education, teacher salaries, incarceration rates, number of farms, etc. These tables of rankings are noteworthy because of the significant number of requests librarians constantly receive for a ranking of a state in relation to other states. (It is easier for legislators to argue for funding for a specific program or service if their state ranks last or near the bottom in comparison to other states.)

Book of the States (Council of State Governments, Lexington, KY) Biennial.

This book examines recent activities and changes in state government in nine areas. Those areas are state elections, finances, management and administration, intergovernmental affairs, selected state issues, the state executive, judicial and legislative branches, and the state constitutions. Over 200 information tables are well placed throughout this book. Both the statistical data and review of trends make this book a valuable resource. The book also contains a section titled "State Pages," which provides some ready reference information on each state, including the capitol city of the state, the telephone number of its central switchboard, and basic statistics. A subject index is also included.

City and County Data Book (U.S. Bureau of the Census, U.S. Dept. of Commerce, U.S. Government Printing Office, Washington, DC) Irregular.

A wonderful statistical resource, the *Data Book* provides information on states, counties, cities (with over 25,000 people), and places with over 25,000 inhabitants in a variety of subjects ranging from vital statistics to housing and trade. The book is divided into four sections called tables. Tables A, B, and C contain data in the same topical areas, but Table A presents figures for the states, Table B for the counties, and Table C for cities. The last table, Table D, contains population and income statistics for all places with 2500 or more inhabitants. The book also contains other data such as rankings of counties by selected subjects, a list of county search, maps, and more. The book is a supplement to the *U.S. Statistical Abstract*.

City Fiscal Conditions in (Year) (National League of Cities, Washington, DC) Annual.

A survey of city fiscal conditions, this publication examines city revenues and expenditures, budgets, and employment. Any new trends are highlighted in this survey.

Condition of Education (U.S. Dept. of Education, Office of Educational Research and Improvement, National Center for Education Statistics, Washington, DC) Annual.

Divided into two volumes, volume one "presents 29 indicators on the state of elementary and secondary education in the United States." These indicators range from public school revenues and expenditures per pupil in public schools to dropout rates, and student substance abuse statistics. Volume two focuses on postsecondary education and includes indicators ranging from the number of degrees earned to student characteristics and human resources.

Digest of Education Statistics (U.S. Dept. of Education, National Center for Education Statistics, Washington, DC) Annual.

This digest provides statistics on the American educational system from kindergarten to graduate school. These statistics include information such as the number of schools and colleges, the number of teachers, the number of colleges awarding degrees in each field, the proportion of high school graduates going to college, and a wealth of other figures.

Elected Officials Handbooks (Washington, DC, ICMA) 3rd edition. 1988.

Consisting of five handbooks, this set provides an overview of government functions and also discusses how governments are dealing with common issues. Handbook one focuses on setting goals for action, handbook two on building a policy-making team, handbook three on setting policies for service delivery, handbook four on setting policies for internal management, and handbook five on pursuing personal effectiveness. The handbooks are written to be of use to both newly elected and experienced officials.

Inside the Legislative Process (American Society of Legislative Clerks and Secretaries in cooperation with the National Conference of State Legislatures, Denver, CO) May 1992.

This survey of state legislative clerks and secretaries contains detailed information on the following seven topics: (1) general legislative procedures, such as legislative organization and sessions, (2) committee procedures pertaining to consideration of bills, committee reports, notices of meetings, etc., (3) the processing of bills, from their reading to debate, (4) public information issues ranging from the taping of sessions to the indexing of bills, (5) legislative documents, (6) information about the Office of Chief Clerk and Secretary containing information from selection of Chamber Officers, staff functions, parliamentary authority, etc., and (7) personnel policies including data on fringe benefits, leave plans, etc. In addition to survey data, brief discussions of some trends and practices in legislative procedures and operations are also included.

Leaders' Outlook: Top Priorities for State Legislatures (National Conference of State Legislatures, Denver, CO) Annual.

This publication is based on responses to surveys sent to state legislative leaders regarding their top priorities and issues. The top priorities are identified and summarized.

Mason's Manual of Legislative Procedure, by the American Society of Legislative Clerks and Secretaries in cooperation with the National Conference of State Legislatures (West Publishing Company, St. Paul, MN) 1989.

Evolving from a study of legislative precedents and practice, and judicial decisions, this manual provides information on the rules of parliamentary law, plus procedures and practices of administrative bodies and voluntary associations.

The Municipal Yearbook (International City Management Association, Washington, DC) Annual.

The yearbook presents articles and descriptive statistics on staffing, management, intergovernmental relations, and other municipal concerns. Several statistical tables appear throughout the yearbook. Most of the data for these tables was acquired through questionnaires completed by public officials. The yearbook also includes a section devoted to directory information on U.S. municipal and county officials, state association of counties, state municipal leagues, and other potential sources of municipal information.

Politics in America (Congressional Quarterly Inc., Washington, DC) Biennial.

This book is much more than just a biographical sourcebook. It presents profiles, photographs, and political assessments of senators and representatives both in Washington and in their home districts. The assessments of the congresspersons were arrived at "by watching them in action, by conducting interviews with their peers and by researching the public record." In addition, each profile includes a half-page description of the legislator's congressional district, committees the congressperson serves on, general election and other returns for the congressperson's most recent general election, previous winning percentages, campaign finance receipts and expenditures for the two-year election cycle, key votes, interest group ratings, plus scores representing the percentage of time a member has supported or opposed a party, presidential or Conservative Coalition position.

The information is arranged by state, then by Senate and House members. The beginning of each state section includes a map of the congressional districts in the state and a page of brief state statistics.

The book also includes a photograph and brief profile of the delegates from Guam, the Virgin Islands, American Samoa, and Puerto Rico, and a list of House, Senate, and Joint Committees. Also present is a seniority list of House and Senate Members, plus a very helpful pronunciation guide for the most often mispronounced names of congressional members.

Protocol: The Complete Handbook of Diplomatic, Official and Social Usage, by Mary Jane McCaffree and Pauline Innis (Devon Publishing Co., Washington, DC) 1985.

This guide to proper diplomatic protocol is used at both the White House and the State Department. It contains pertinent information such as the order of precedence for ranking officials, proper invitations and replies for various occasions, proper table seating arrangements, flag etiquette and ceremonies, and many other aspects of protocol that should be observed by government officials.

Significant Features of Fiscal Federalism (Advisory Commission on Intergovernmental Relations, U.S. Government Printing Office, Washington, DC) Annual.

This is a convenient compendium of information relating to tax rates, the budget processes, and revenue and expenditures of federal, state, and local governments in the U.S. Over 100 tables present information ranging from property taxes, and excise taxes and fees, to government expenditures and state fiscal rankings. The three basic sources from which the data is drawn are the Census, national income statistics, and the federal budget.

State and Metropolitan Area Data Book (U.S. Dept. of Commerce, Bureau of the Census, U.S. Government Printing Office, Washington, DC) Irregular.

A supplement to the *U.S. Statistical Abstract,* the book contains statistical data on states and metropolitan areas in topics such as health, income, education, and population.

State Issues: A Survey of Priority Issues in State Legislatures (National Conference of State Legislatures, Denver, CO) Annual.

The priority issues of each state, and of the states in general, are reported in this publication. The information is presented in 18 topical sections, with each section containing an introduction to the topic written by an NCSL specialist, and charts illustrating state-by-state priorities, and the national priority level. The information is derived from surveys sent to 44 state legislatures.

State Legislative Sourcebook (Government Research Service, Topeka, KS) Annual.

This looseleaf reference work serves as a guide to legislative information in all 50 states plus Puerto Rico. It contains information on the number of members in each legislature, terms of office, and lengths of sessions. Its strength, however, lies in the contact information it provides. By consulting the sourcebook you can find out who or where to contact for copies of bills, legislative journals, enactments, slip laws, bill histories, committee rosters, and much more. For instance, it also lists the telephone number to call in each state for the status of a bill. Or, if you're interested in the politics or organization of a specific legislature, the sourcebook presents references to relevant books, videos, and summaries. The sourcebook is arranged by state.

States in Profile: The State Policy Reference Book (Brizius & Foster and State Policy Research Inc., McConnellsburg, PA) Annual.

Primarily a statistical reference source, *States in Profile* contains data in all areas relating to state policy decisions, such as spending and employment, taxes, education, social services, etc. Most of the 200-plus tables in this volume rank the states accordingly. Each table also contains a national average for the specific data covered in that table. This information can be used not only to find a ranking of a state in a specific area, but also to help measure the effectiveness and productivity of state governments.

State Rankings (Morgan Quitno, Lawrence, KS) Annual.

If you are looking for information on how a state ranks in comparison to others, be sure to check this resource. It contains comparative statistical information in over 450 categories ranging from highway fatality rates to lottery payouts. The information is presented in neat, easy-to-use tables.

A Uniform System of Citation (Harvard Law Review Association, Cambridge, MA).

This book is a must for anyone citing legal materials. It contains general rules of citation, technical rules of citation pertaining to cases, statutes, foreign legal materials, and other forms of authority. Lists of abbreviations of various codes and reporters for both the U.S. and other countries are included as well.

Legal Materials

"Ignorance of the law excuses no man," wrote the sixteenth-century English jurist John Selden. Ignorance of existing laws is especially unpardonable for individuals involved in enacting or changing those laws. Persons involved in the legislative process must have access to basic legal materials. These materials will only be mentioned here in a general fashion since the purpose of this section is to highlight materials useful to legislative reference staff. Bibliographic citations of the items are generally not provided since there are often various editions and publishers of the same information. More detailed information on legal reference and research can be found in several other published works.

The best place to begin addressing legal materials is with the statutes. *Statutes* are enactments, or bills that become laws, of the U.S. Congress and state legislatures. They are often cumulated in publications such as *Statutes at Large,* the official compilation of Congressional enactments published each legislative session by the Office of the Federal Register. More frequently they are compiled by subject into volumes commonly known as *codes* or *code sets,* like the *U.S. Code, Florida Code,* etc. Individual volumes within code sets are often referred to by the topic, like the *California Penal Code.* The laws enacted at the local government level by city councils and other legislative bodies are referred to as *ordinances.*

Congress, state legislatures, and other government legislative bodies also delegate some legislative functions to government agencies. The laws drafted by these agencies are referred to as *regulations.* At the federal level, regulations are cumulated and published in the *Code of Federal Regulations.* As new ones are enacted, they are announced and appear in the *Federal Register.*

At the state level, regulations are often not cumulated. If they are, the titles of these cumulations vary. They are often referred to as state codes of regulations or state administrative codes. Regulations drafted at the local government level often are not cumulated and published; they are usually maintained by a designated city or county office, but they are not "published" per se.

Another entity with the authority to enact laws is the executive office, i.e., the President, state governors, and city mayors. They can enact *executive orders* and *proclamations.* Proclamations are often enacted for a limited time and are of an honorary nature. Executive orders, however, carry a significant legal impact. At the federal level, executive orders can have significant legal impacts in domestic and foreign affairs. They will appear in the *Federal Regis-*

ter, Code of Federal Regulations, and other publications. At the state and local level, executive orders can have profound effects on their appropriate jurisdictions. At this level, they are usually distributed as appropriate and maintained and filed in a state or local government office or agency.

Although the courts do not draft laws, their decisions affect the legal system by interpreting those laws that have been enacted. Referred to as *case law,* they are published in series known as *reporters* by a variety of legal publishers. Reporters are useful in locating legal precedence. Cases are usually arranged in the reporters chronologically. And most reporters have a table of cases in each individual volume. More comprehensive indexing can be found in *digests.* As indexes to case law, digests will also provide subject access to the cases.

It is essential that legislative reference staff have access to the following legal materials:

- Constitution of the U.S.
- state constitution (for state legislative reference bureaus)
- federal and state statutes
- federal and state digest of legislation
- federal and state bills
- federal and state administrative rules
- federal and state legislative opinions
- federal and state court opinions
- advisory opinions
- federal and state legislative rules
- national and state legal encyclopedia (if available)

Other legal related materials that legislative staff should have easy access to are:

- bill drafting manual
- legal citation manual
- legal dictionary
- legislative journals (federal and state)
- legislative rules
- legislative calendars
- legal research handbook

Other legal materials of particular interest appear below:

American Jurisprudence 2d (Lawyers Co-Operative Publishing Company, Rochester, NY and Bancroft-Whitney Co., San Francisco, CA) 1962-
A legal encyclopedia, it provides a general introduction to major legal topics in the Anglo-American legal system. Updated by pocket parts, it also contains an index.

Corpus Juris Secundum (West Publishing Co., St. Paul, MN) 1936-
Similar to *American Jurisprudence*, this encyclopedia also attempts to restate American law in an encyclopedic format. It differs from *American Jurisprudence* in that it cites all reported cases in support of its textual statements of the law. This publication is also updated by pocket parts.

Martindale-Hubbell Law Directory (Martindale-Hubbell Law Directory Inc., Washington, DC) Annual.
This multi-volume directory covers the legal profession across the nation. Each individual volume is divided into three sections: Practice Profiles, Professional Biographies, and Services and Suppliers. The Practice Profiles Section contains attorney rosters for the various U.S. and Canadian Bar Associations. Professional biographies, including the firm name, brief personal biographical data, areas of practice, representative clients, and references are included in the second section. The last section contains information on suppliers of goods and services that support the legal profession. The entries in each section are grouped by state, then arranged alphabetically by city, then by personal name or name of the firm.

Selected State Enactments: A 50-State Survey of Enacted Legislation of Priority Issues (National Conference of State Legislatures, Denver, CO) Annual.
This publication identifies recently enacted legislation in approximately 20 topic areas. This 50-state survey is intended to assist users who may be investigating the topical subject areas included in the compendium. Its information is derived from over 900 survey responses.

Subject Compilations of State Laws, 1988-1990 (C. Boast and C. Nyberg, Urbana, IL); 1985-1988 (C. Boast and C. Nyberg, Urbana, IL); 1983-1985 (C. Boast and C. Nyberg, Urbana, IL); 1979-1983 (Greenwood Press, Westport, CT); 1960-1979 (Greenwood Press, Westport, CT).

These annotated bibliographies list thousands of legal periodicals, looseleaf services, court opinions, books, and federal and state government documents that compare state laws on hundreds of subjects from whistle-blowing to foster care. The entries in each book are arranged by subject, then alphabetically by author or title. The books are very useful when starting a 50-state survey on the law of a specific topic.

U.S. Law Week (Bureau of National Affairs, Washington, DC) Weekly.

Timely information pertaining to the U.S. Supreme Court can be found in this publication. The text of U.S. Supreme Court decisions are published the day after the case is decided. In addition, this looseleaf contains a calendar of hearings scheduled, summaries of cases recently filed, cases docketed, and appropriate indices.

Words and Phrases (West Publishing Co., St. Paul, MN) 1964.

This multi-volume set lists thousands of words and phrases and their interpretation by state and federal courts. The words and phrases are arranged alphabetically. The volumes are updated by supplemental pocket parts.

Journals and Periodicals

Journals devoted to issues of governmental concern can be useful sources of information when responding to legislative requests. Library staff can also stay abreast of current topics of governmental interest by scanning the table of contents of these journals on a regular basis. Reading the journals is always desirable, but few of us are afforded the luxury of sufficient time to do so.

Many of these journals, however, are read by legislative staff and members on a regular basis. The majority of these publications are targeted to readers involved in the legislative or governing process. Because of their specialization, not all of these journals are indexed in commercial services. Whenever possible, information on the indexing of a specific journal is listed in the following list of journals.

General Interest Publications

The following journals contain articles of interest to government leaders, officials, and employees in all fields. They cover a wide variety of topics of current concern at various levels of government.

American City and County (Communication Channels Inc., Atlanta, GA) Monthly (ISSN 0149-337X).
Privatization and recycling are just two of the many topics that have been discussed in this magazine. Articles in this journal focus on trends and issues in local government.

Brookings Review (Brookings Institution, Washington, DC) Quarterly (ISSN 0745-1253).
The Review contains articles on economic, political, and public policy issues. A sample of recent articles focused on topics such as the cost-effectiveness of imprisonment, and free trade.

Congressional Quarterly Weekly Report (Congressional Quarterly Inc., Washington, DC) Weekly (ISSN 0010-5910).
Each week this publication reports and analyzes significant congressional and political activities. It provides a good summary of the events and issues that have transpired, as well as presenting information on the status of major bills before Congress. The full text of presidential statements and speeches are often included in this publication. A subject index is included in each issue, with a cumulative index published on an annual basis.

County News (National Association of Counties, Washington, DC) Biweekly (ISSN 0744-9798).
The publication reports on county news of interest to the association's members.

Governing (Congressional Quarterly, Washington, DC) Monthly (ISSN 0894-3842).
Written for people involved in state government, or lower levels of government, this journal highlights effective techniques of governing, successful government programs, and various topics of interest to state and local officials and employees. (The journal is selectively indexed in the *PAIS Bulletin*.)

Government Executive (National Journal Inc., Washington, DC) Monthly (ISSN 0017-2626).

Articles in this magazine cover a wide range of topics of interest to government administrators. Regular departments appearing in this magazine include Management Focus Profile and Information Technology.

Governors' Weekly Bulletin (National Governors' Association, Washington, DC) Weekly (ISSN 0888-8647).

This newsletter presents information on National Governors' Association initiatives, projects, and policies.

ICMA Newsletter (ICMA, Washington, DC) Biweekly (ISSN 0047-0651).

An association newsletter, it reports on news and activities of, and of interest to the ICMA. It also includes information on job vacancies and job appointments in local government.

Intergovernmental Relations (U.S. Advisory Commission on Intergovernmental Relations, Washington, DC) Quarterly.

Various issues in federal, state, and local government relations are addressed in this publication. A recent article, for example, focused on the successful establishment of state advisory commissions on intergovernmental relations.

Leaders' Outlook (Year): Top Priorities for State Legislatures (National Conference of State Legislatures, Denver, CO) Annual.

Based on survey responses, the publication highlights the top three priorities in the states and also briefly lists other priorities frequently noted.

Nation's Cities Weekly (National League of Cities, Washington, DC) Weekly (ISSN 0164-5935).

Distributed to members of the League, this weekly newspaper reports on Congressional, state, or court actions that affect cities. It also looks at innovative approaches taken by some cities to solve the problems facing today's municipalities.

National Civic Review (National Civic League, Denver, CO) Quarterly (ISSN 0027-9013).

Innovations in local government are examined in this publication, which is indexed in be *PAIS* and other commercial indices.

National Journal: The Weekly on Politics and Government (National Journal Inc., Washington, DC) Weekly.

This journal presents feature articles pertaining to government, politics, and the powerful players. It provides news summaries and in-depth reports on new trends or topics of significant importance. It gives readers a non-partisan look at the policy-making process.

The Political Animal: The National Letter (Political Animal Ltd., Torrance, CA) Biweekly (ISSN 0747-5659).

Approximately four pages in length, this newsletter provides information and commentary of politics at the national level.

Public Affairs Report (Institute of Governmental Studies, University of California, Berkeley, CA) Bimonthly (ISSN 0033-3417).

This publication reports on politics and public policy. It is produced by the Institute of Governmental Studies at U.C. Berkeley, which conducts research on public policy, public administration, politics, urban problems, and related areas.

Public Management (ICMA, Washington, DC) Monthly (ISSN 0033-3611).

Focusing on topics of interest to local government, this journal contains articles highlighting successful methods of dealing with matters of mutual concern. Each issue focuses on a theme such as "Keeping Budgets (and Credit Ratings) on Tract" and "Environmental Challenges for the 90s."

Reapportionment Law Update (National Conference of State Legislatures, Denver, CO) Quarterly (ISSN 1050-0235).

This newsletter focuses on bills, initiatives, and court cases dealing with or impacting redistricting. News about reapportionment meetings and other activities are also included.

Roll Call: The Newspaper of Capitol Hill (Levitt Communications Inc., Washington, DC) Published twice a week (ISSN 0035-788X).

Roll Call reports on news pertaining to congressional issues, members, the Executive Office, and other matters of interest pertaining to Capitol Hill.

State and Local Government Review (Carol Vinson Institute of Government, University of Georgia, Athens, GA) Triennial (ISSN 0160-323X).

"The purpose of the *Review* is to provide an interchange of ideas for practitioners and academics on applied research, training, and policy making in state and local government." Each issue includes articles focusing on a particular topic for that issue (such as judicial administration or local government finances), and articles on various topics appear in their "Practitioner's Corner." The articles in the journal are well written, easy to read, and the information is nicely presented. (Indexed in *PAIS*, *Political Science Abstracts*, other indexes, and selectively in the LEGISNET System.)

State Government News (Council of State Governments, Denver, CO) Monthly (ISSN 0039-0119).

In addition to covering events and developments in the states, this journal also looks at innovative programs in state government. Every issue includes the "Targeted Innovations" column that briefly describes innovative programs and provides the program contact should further information be desired. Another nice feature of the magazine is its "Point/Counterpoint" department in which two viewpoints are presented on topics ranging from whether pesticide taxes would hurt farmers, to whether or not the initiative process is a good idea. (The publication in indexed in the *PAIS Bulletin*, *Management Contents*, and other indexes.)

State Government Research Checklist (Council of State Governments, Lexington, KY) Bimonthly.

This is basically a list of new acquisitions to the Council of State Governments' library available on loan to Council constituents. Most of the acquisitions are federal and state legislative, executive, judicial, agency, or Council publications. The Checklist provides a means for awareness and an aid in collection development of new public policy literature.

State Legislatures (National Conference of State Legislatures, Denver, CO) Monthly (ISSN 0147-6041).

Targeted to and read by state legislative staff, members of Congress, and governors, *State Legislatures* features articles on issues being addressed in the various states, or federal issues of state concern. The journal also contains a "Stateline" column that provides news briefs on actions or new programs in the states. It provides a nice timely roundup of what is occurring at the state level across the nation. (Indexed in the LEGISNET System.)

Legislative Studies Quarterly (Comparative Legislative Research Center, Iowa City, IA) Quarterly (ISSN 0362-9805).

The articles in this journal examine various aspects of state and local legislatures, the U.S. Congress, and in some instances, foreign legislatures. The articles accentuate electoral and legislative studies. (The journal is indexed in several sources, including *U.S. Political Science Documents* and *Political Science Abstracts.*)

Mandate Watch List (National Conference of State Legislatures, Denver, CO) Ten to 12 issues per year.

This publication is intended to alert readers to pending legislation containing federal mandates on state and local government. The list contains the bill number, sponsor, brief title, explanation and programs affected, and the status of the bill.

Background Publications

The publications listed below are geared toward providing background or briefing information on a variety of timely topics.

Congressional Digest (Congressional Digest Corp., Washington, DC) Monthly (ISSN 0010-5899).

Readers of this digest will find a good introduction to controversial issues facing Congress. Each issue provides several pages of background information on a specific controversy, followed by the pros and cons of the issue presented by members of Congress or individuals associated with the topic. The digest has devoted issues to controversies such as the Brady Handgun Violence Protection Act, Persian Gulf Policies, the Family and Medical Leave Act, and a variety of other issues addressed by Congress.

CSG Backgrounder (Council of State Governments, Lexington, KY) Monthly.

Each monthly issue provides background information on current topics such as banning out-of-state waste. This publication is very similar to the *State Legislative Report.*

State-Federal Issue Briefs (National Conference of State Legislatures, Denver, CO) Irregular.

Each briefing report focuses on a specific federal issue affecting state government. For example, past issues have focused on topics such as the Clean Air Act Amendments of 1990 and the tax treatment of public utilities.

State Legislative Report (National Conference of State Legislatures, Denver, CO) Irregular (12 to 18 issues per year).

Each issue presents a brief overview of a specific topic of concern to the states. Each report usually runs between five to 15 pages long. Recent issues have focused on state cutback management, compensated worksharing, and asbestos removal. This publication is distributed free to legislative leaders, council and research directors, and legislative librarians.

Financial and Business Publications

Finance and economics are an ongoing concern at all levels of government. This concern is demonstrated by the number of journals devoted specifically to this topic. Following are some commonly read publications in this area.

City and State (Crain Communications Inc., Chicago, IL) Semimonthly. (ISSN 0885-940X).

The "business newspaper" covers the business aspects of state and local governments. It features a "Government Manager" section that presents information on specific topics of interest to managers, such as information technology, or recycling services. Recent issues of *City and State* have included articles such as "Biting the Budget Bullet: Tax Hikes Seen as Solution for States' Troubles" and "Help Wanted for JTPA Flop: States Fail in Oversight of Federal Job Training."

Federal Update (National Conference of State Legislatures, Washington, DC) Bimonthly (ISSN 0898-4298).

A newsletter, it reports on state tax, budget, and other fiscal issues from a national perspective. Statistical information pertaining to trends or comparative state data frequently appear in this publication. Each news entry contains the name of the NCSL contact person should you desire further information.

The Fiscal Letter (National Conference of State Legislatures, Denver, CO) Monthly (ISSN 0197-288X).

This newsletter focuses on taxation and spending in the states. Each issue reports on various government finance issues in the states. The newsletter provides a good overview of issues at the state level, and frequently contains 50-state survey charts. (It is indexed in the LEGISNET System).

Fiscal Survey of the States (National Governors' Association and National Association of State Budget Officers, Washington, DC) Annual (ISSN 1-55877-0666).

This survey provides information on the states' expenditures, general fund revenues, and balances. It presents 50-state survey tables of fiscal data where appropriate, while providing an aggregate overview of developments in each area. Data for this publication is gathered from surveys completed by the Governors' state budget officers.

Government Finance Review (Government Finance Officers Association of the U.S. and Canada, Chicago, IL) Bimonthly.

Distributed to members of the Government Finance Officers Association, the magazine looks at the practice and management of finances at the state and local level. It provides a timely look at issues of interest to practicing finance officers. (*The Review* is indexed in the *PAIS Bulletin*, ABI INFORM, and the *Business Periodicals Index.*)

Journal of State Government (Council of State Governments, Lexington, KY) Quarterly (ISSN 0039-0097).

The articles in this journal analyze diverse political, social, and economic issues of interest to state government officials. Each issue focuses on a specific theme such as women in state politics, health care issues, etc.

Kiplinger Washington Newsletter (Kiplinger Washington Editors, Washington, DC) Weekly (ISSN 0023-1770).

This newsletter reads like a letter to a business client. It analyzes and summarizes government activities affecting business, and reports on business trends.

Municipal Finance Journal (Panel Publishers Inc., New York, NY) Quarterly (ISSN 0199-6134).

Despite its title, the journal addresses current financial issues at the municipal, county, and state level. Emphasis is placed on the legal, political, and economic aspects of the management, acquisition, and allocation of fiscal resources. (Indexed in the *Legal Periodicals Index, Management Contents,* and others.)

State Policy Reports (State Policy Research Inc., Alexandria, VA) Semi-monthly (ISSN 8750-6637).

This publication reports and analyzes state policies pertaining to economic issues. A significant feature of this publication is the 50-state comparison charts contained in most issues.

Up to this point various materials specifically targeted at legislative users or containing information of specific legislative interest have been cited. A number of other materials should also be include in a legislative reference collection. These materials include:

- an almanac
- a bible
- a bill drafting manual
- a book of quotations
- a business directory
- the Constitution of the U.S.
- a dictionary (unabridged)
- a directory of associations
- a directory of Congress (preferably with brief biographical data)
- a directory of federal agencies and officials
- a directory of state government agencies and officials
- a directory of county government agencies and officials
- a directory of local government agencies and officials
- a directory of the media
- an encyclopedia
- a guide to parliamentary procedure
- a law dictionary
- a legal citation manual
- a legal research guide
- legislative calendars
- maps of legislative districts
- a medical dictionary
- a medical handbook

- a publishers directory
- a secretary's handbook
- a statistical handbook
- a state bluebook
- a style manual

NONPRINT RESOURCES

Associations

Organizations of governments and government officials are superb resources of information. Their members shape and run governments, their staff are public policy experts and researchers, their publications are indispensable, and their overall knowledge of the process and politics that shape government policy are beyond reproach. This section will acquaint you with selective associations that serve, or are comprised of government officials, and are valuable resources of information. The purpose of the association, as well as the services it provides to its members, will be briefly reviewed.

Council of State Governments

"The mission of The Council of State Governments is to provide state elected and appointed officials with information and strategies needed to develop and implement public policy." To this end the council promotes cooperative government ventures and partnerships within and between state government and business and academia, while identifying and shaping strategies to meet tomorrow's challenges. It collects, analyzes, and disseminates information needed by the states. Much of these activities have resulted in numerous publications ranging from multi-state surveys to guidebooks. Other activities are targeted at producing publications, for example the Council's Committee on Suggested State Legislation annually selects draft legislation published in *Suggested State Legislation.*

Another strength of the council lies in the information services it provides to its members. State administrative, legislative, and judicial officials have access to the State Information Center, which furnishes answers to questions about state government issues. To enable them to answer these questions, the council polls the states for data and then maintains files of this information on over 300 major topics. Their information center actively collects information and maintains over 10,000 reports and documents, which can be borrowed for 30 days. To facilitate access to their collection, members can request access to the Council's Integrated States Information System (ISIS), an online information system containing records of materials held in the information center, plus articles from *State Government News* and selective other council publications.

The council is very active in publishing materials of interest to the states. They produce valuable works such as the *State Elective Officials and The Legislatures* directory, and the *Books of the States* to the 1990 *Final Report and Recommendations of the National Commission to Restructure the Interstate Compact for the Supervision of Parolees and Probationers*. Their periodicals include *State Government News*, and the *Journal of State Government* in addition to a number of other titles. Overall, the council is an excellent source for information on state government and state government issues.

ICMA–The Professional Local Government Association

"The purpose of the ICMA is to enhance the quality of local government and to support and assist local government professionals in the United States and other countries." The ICMA's membership consists primarily of appointed chief administrative officers and assistants in cities, counties, towns, townships, and villages. The membership also includes local government employees and others interested in quality local government.

Members of the association can take advantage of a variety of services and benefits offered by the ICMA, such as training programs, registration discounts off their annual conference, and access to local government data on a variety of topics. Members receive *Public Management* magazine and the *ICMA Newsletter*, in addition to the annual membership directory. The ICMA also publishes other materials like their recent publications *Citizen Surveys:*

How to Do Them, How to Use Them, What They Mean and the *Commercial/Industrial Water Conservation Guide.*

National Association of Counties

The purpose of the National Association of Counties (NACo (440 First St., N.W. Washington, DC 20001, 202-393-6226)) is to (1) serve as a liaison with other levels of government, (2) to improve public understanding of counties, (3) to act as an advocate for counties before Congress, and (4) to assist counties in meeting the challenges they face. NACo's membership consists of county governments of all sizes, and NACo provides its members with numerous services. These services include providing information about federal grants and aid available to counties, and providing technical assistance in areas such as mental health and transportation. NACo also promotes a better understanding of counties through continuous public affairs activities, while it represents and acts as an advocate for counties. On an annual basis, NACo sponsors a conference and several workshops on issues facing counties. The association also publishes and distributes *County News* to its members.

National Association of Towns and Townships

The association provides technical assistance to its members and sponsors training sessions and an annual conference. It also conducts research of various topics and provides guides and videotapes to meet the needs of its members.

National Conference of State Legislatures

The National Conference of State Legislatures' (NCSL) members consist of state legislators and state legislative staff. The aim of NCSL is "to improve the quality and effectiveness of state legislatures, to foster interstate communication and cooperation, and to ensure legislatures a strong, cohesive voice in the federal system."

Members benefit from numerous educational, informational, and professional services provided by NCSL. NCSL sponsors workshops for legislative staff focusing on skills ranging from bill drafting to public relations with the press. On an annual basis they present a management seminar and another seminar to help new staff people refine their legislative skills. And every two years they conduct a Symposium for New Leaders that addresses leadership skills, the legislative process, and policy development. The Conference also schedules meetings on various topics, and holds an annual conference each summer.

NCSL also provides excellent information services and assistance to its members. The Conference employs a staff of research specialists in a variety of subject areas to respond to questions, provide expert advice, and to research topics. Their research staff utilizes NCSL's library containing over 3,000 volumes and the LEGISNET system.

Operated by NCSL, LEGISNET is an online database accessible by its members. It contains abstracts of journal articles, documents, and legislative reports, in addition to uniform model acts and other information. NCSL likewise is a strong publisher of books pertaining to state government issues. Their publication subjects run the gamut from budget procedures in the 50 states to the economic impact of the arts. Reference books published by NCSL include the *Directory of Legislative Leaders*, the *State Legislative Staff Directory*, and *State Policy Abstracts*. The Conference also publishes *The Fiscal Letter, State Legislatures*, and other periodicals as well as a series of video and audio tapes. NCSL is definitely an information source not to be ignored.

National Governor's Association

Besides representing the governors' interests before Congress, this association provides its members with training and technical assistance in policy and program development. It conducts research and disseminates pertinent information through seminars, conferences, and various publications. The association publishes a number of reports, and also issues an annual directory of governors', and governors' staff. They also publish the *Governors' Weekly Bulletin* and *Federal Funds Information for States Newsletter*.

National League of Cities

Comprised of over 1,300 communities, the League represents municipal government and its interest before Congress. The organization analyzes, evaluates, and comments upon proposed or existing policies or legislation affecting cities. To keep its members informed, the League publishes and distributes *Nation's Cities Weekly*, which reports on events of interest to local government officials. It also maintains a library and municipal reference services available to officials of member cities. And in terms of educational activities, the League sponsors seminars and an annual conference.

One of the League's many strengths is its publications program. In addition to its weekly newspaper, they also publish the monthly *Urban Affairs Abstracts* and numerous other publications in topics ranging from economic development to land use planning. Recent titles include *AIDS in the Workplace: Municipal Policies Affecting Safety and Personnel* and *Local Officials Guide to Public Real Estate Asset Management*.

Chapter 5

Online Resources

The flourishing online industry currently provides a variety of online databases and systems particularly useful in legislative reference. These online resources contain information ranging from the status of federal and state bills, to abstracts of public policy literature. This chapter is intended to alert and acquaint the librarian with specific online resources useful in his or her work. But first, the pros and cons of retrieving information from an online system will be reviewed.

PROS

Speed

Attempts to locate information with an incomplete citation could take hours in a manual search. All too often patrons will walk or call in an incomplete or erroneous citation to an item they need as soon as possible. With access to an appropriate online database, the needed information can be retrieved within minutes.

Currency of Information

Online databases provide access to current information frequently before the library acquires it in print. For example, the text of U.S. Supreme Court decisions impacting all levels of government can be retrieved from an online source days before the printed copy is received in the mail. Some news databases are even updated as often as every 15 minutes. The ability to access timely information is extremely useful in responding to requests for information on current events, such as current floods, fires, earthquakes, strikes, etc., in a legislator's home district.

Increased Access Points

Online databases also provide more access points to information than conventional print indices. Most print indices provide only author, title, or subject indexing. Online resources can provide additional access points, including the ability to search for words within the title, abstract, or text of the information. Your search can also be limited by language, geographical area, type of information, and a variety of other qualifiers. The ability to search for words or phrases anywhere in the text is another powerful tool when searching for obscure names of topics.

Ability to Link Concepts

Online databases also allow users to link concepts from different disciplines into a singe topic search. For example, if you are seeking information on the relation between children living at the poverty level and their academic performance, the concepts of poverty, academic performance, and elementary school grades can be easily linked together in an online search. Whereas it would be extremely difficult and time consuming in a manual review of the literature.

CONS

Although online databases and systems greatly facilitate our work, they do have their drawbacks. Some of these are listed below.

Cost

Access to most online services is not free. Users are charged online connect time rates ranging from approximately $35 per hour to $300 per hour, plus an additional charge for each record printed or displayed. Other services may charge a flat subscription fee with unlimited searching. The government produced or sponsored databases tend to be less expensive than your commercial databases. The most expensive online time rates are generally charged for access to the commercial business databases.

Everything You Seek Is Not Online

Although access to online data can facilitate your work, it can also frustrate you at times. Not everything you expect to be contained in an online source actually is. Online databases may contain the citations or text of thousands of journals, newspapers, and other documents, but they cannot contain everything published in a given field. A number of publications are now on the market that can help you determine whether a specific publication is indexed or contained in an online format. These publications are *BiblioData Fulltext Sources Online*, published by BiblioData of Needham Heights, MA, the *Directory of Periodicals Online*, published by Info Globe, and another directory by the same title published by Federal Document Retrieval Service. You also have to bear in mind that online databases only really began to flourish in the late 1970s. So information published prior to the mid-1970s is seldom indexed online.

No Graphics

Unfortunately, photographs, illustrations, and other graphics contained in articles and other printed works are seldom available in online full-text databases. Although the technology exists, as demonstrated by the TRADEMARKSCAN database accessible through DIALOG Information Services, it has not yet been widely applied. This, however, may change in the near future.

SPECIAL ONLINE LEGISLATIVE RESOURCES

Several special online legislative resources can be invaluable to you in your work. These resources are restricted to certain qualifying users and are generally not accessible by the general public. In most cases, they are designed for specific legislative users. Three of these special resources are the Council of State Governments' Integrated States Information System (ISIS), the National Conference of State Legislatures' LEGISNET system, and the Library of Congress Information System (LOCIS).

Integrated States Information System (ISIS)

The Council of State Governments, a joint agency of state governments, maintains the Integrated States Information System available to authorized executive, judicial, and state legislative users. The system is available 24 hours a day and offers a menu-driven search approach to its STATABASE and BIBLIOFILE databases.

The STATABASE contains the full text of *State Government News* (1988-) and the *Backgrounder* from 1986 to date. Abstracts of prior issues of both titles appear in the STATABASE as well as abstracts of *Suggested State Legislation* and submissions for the Council's Innovations Award.

The BIBLIOFILE database contains bibliographic records for over 9,000 titles available in the Council's library. These records represent the Council's publications, publications by its affiliate organizations, and state and federal publications normally not found in major bibliographic utilities such as OCLC and RLIN. State agencies can contact the Council's library to arrange a 30-day loan of any of the items cited in their database. To facilitate communication with Council staff, ISIS also offers electronic mail capabilities.

LEGISNET

Another special online resource is the LEGISNET system operated by the National Conference of State Legislatures (NCSL). Available 24 hours a day, seven days a week to constituents of NCSL, and Foundation for State Legislatures donors, LEGISNET consists of the Legislative Information System (LIS) database, the Uniform and Model Acts (UMA) database, the Rules and Procedures (RAP) database, and an online index. An electronic memo system is also available to facilitate requests for documents referenced in the LIS database.

Searchers of the LIS database will find references to state legislative research and program evaluation reports, plus a variety of state and federal executive agency publications. The database also references NCSL's *State Legislatures*, the *Fiscal Letter, Reapportionment Technology Update*, and the *Reapportionment Law Update*. A new file of information focusing on alternative funding mechanisms for state and local environmental programs is presently being added to the database, and should be an excellent source for information on the topic once it is available.

The Uniform and Model Acts database provides access to information on over 130 acts promulgated by the National Conference of Commissioners on Uniform State Laws. For acts numbering under 50 pages, both a summary and the full text of the act are available. For those over 50 pages, an outline of the sections that comprise the act and full bibliographic information can be retrieved and displayed.

The Rules and Procedures database contains the full text of the rules and procedures for the chambers of all 50 of the state legislatures. The database is updated as needed.

Searching LEGISNET requires knowledge of its command language and search structure. Training sessions are held at various locations throughout the year, and a substantial user manual is also available.

Library of Congress Information System (LOCIS)

Walk-in patrons of the Library of Congress and congressional staff have long had the privilege of being able to access the Library of Congress Information System. Now, state libraries and the general public can access LOCIS through the INTERNET. Access is available to both the LOCIS SCORPIO and MUMS systems.

Within the SCORPIO (Subject Content Oriented Retriever for Processing Information) system, searchers can access data in six different files, each with its own focus. One set of basic searching commands is used in all of the files. These commands are simple and make retrieval of data fairly easy. Additional commands are available in specific files like the Legislative Information File.

The Legislative Information File contains information on the status of federal legislation from 1983 to date. Updated on a daily basis, the files can be searched by bill number or title, subject terms, sponsor, committee of referral, and when appropriate, public law number. The files use the same subject terms as those used in the Bibliographic Citation File.

The Bibliographic Citation File is comprised of citations to selected articles, government publications, pamphlets, and other materials dealing with public policy. Each citation contains a brief abstract of the item prepared by the Congressional Research Service staff. The file is updated weekly, and can be searched by author, title, subject, and source of publication.

If the information sought cannot be located in the Bibliographic Citation File, expert information may need to be sought. The National Referral Center Master File is an online directory listing thousands of qualified individuals and organizations willing to provide information to the general public. These experts address primarily scientific, technological, and social science disciplines. The online records for the experts include full contact information, services provided, and any fees that may be involved. The file is updated twice a month.

Updated on a weekly basis is the Copyright History Monographs and Documents Files, which contain information on the copyright registrations for works (excluding periodicals) registered since 1978. Access to the information is by name of the author, claimant, title, or registration number. Information contained in these files is also now available in the U.S. Copyrights Database accessible through DIALOG Information Services.

Other files accessible in the SCORPIO system include the Library of Congress Computerized Catalog (LCCC) and the PRE-MARC file. Both files contain bibliographic citations to books cataloged by the Library of Congress. The LCCC file contains records for English language books cataloged since 1968, French books since 1973, other Western European languages since 1976, Romanized Cyrillic and South Asian languages since 1979, and other non-Roman languages since 1980. Citations for books cataloged prior to those contained in the LCCC file can be found in the PREMARC file. In addition, the PREMARC file also contains records for serials prior to 1984. Records in the PREMARC file are brief and unedited. Both the LCCC and PREMARC files can be searched by author, title, Library of Congress subject heading, and partial Library of Congress classification number.

The LCCC and PREMARC files are also searchable in the Multiple Use MARC System (MUMS). MUMS consists of 14 files containing cataloging records of materials ranging from audio-visual materials to Near Eastern language materials. Also included are name and subject authority records. Since MUMS was designed for cataloging purposes, it requires a very structured command language and displays records in an alphabetic main entry order. The ability to search for records in MUMS can be very useful not only for copy cataloging, but for bibliographic verification and identification of information.

From a reference standpoint, however, access to SCORPIO files will prove to be much more useful. Since congressional topics of focus are frequently of interest to state and local governments, the Bibliographic Citation file is a good source for retrieving background information on a wide range of public policy concerns. And because of the potential impact of pending federal legislation at all levels of government, the Legislative Information Files are useful not only for tracking federal bills, but also for retrieving bill summaries and for referencing public law numbers.

ISIS, LEGISNET, and LOCIS are all good sources for locating information in response to legislative requests. They were each originally conceived and designed to meet the information needs of legislative users and have done an excellent job of fulfilling that goal. If you qualify for access to one or more of these systems, I strongly urge you to do so.

BILL TRACKING SYSTEMS

A variety of other online resources can assist you in tracking the status of federal and state bills. Although this information can be found in printed sources, online bill tracking systems give you the convenience of speed and easy access to the information. For congressional, and in some cases state bills, these systems present details of the steps that have been taken on a bill since its introduction, plus information on its current status, such as committee actions. The sponsor of the bill is provided and in some systems, the full text of the bill is also available. Four systems providing online bill tracking are STATENET, LEGI-SLATE, LEGITECH, and Mead Data Central's LEXIS/NEXIS system.

STATENET

STATENET provides information on the status of federal and state bills, as well as forecasts of the probability of passage of congressional bills. STATENET can also supply users with the legislative calendars for all states and the Congress plus directory information on members of the Congress, and members of state legislatures. The system is menu-driven and utilizes a toll-free number.

LEGI-SLATE

The status of congressional bills is a focus of LEGI-SLATE, which offers brief analyses of each bill, summaries of committee amendments, voting records, member profiles, staff directories, and committee schedules. It also provides electronic access to the full text of bills, the *Congressional Record*, the *Federal Register*, the *Code of Federal Regulations*, the *United States Code*, transcripts of selected committee hearings, and selected news interviews as well as *The Washington Post* and *National Journal*. A nice aspect of LEGI-SLATE is its retrospective date coverage. Floor votes, legislative histories, and public interest group ratings of members date back to 1979. The text of bills introduced since the start of the 99th Congress (1985) are likewise available.

LEGITECH

Legi-Tech's Washington On-line Congressional Tracking System follows the status of Congressional bills and allows users to check on not only the status of a bill, but daily events and recorded floor and committee votes as well. The full text of the bills is searchable and retrievable. A useful feature of the Washington Online Systems is your ability to store and sort information in the system. This enables you to produce customized reports as needed. Legi-Tech is a very user-friendly system.

Mead Data Central's LEXIS/NEXIS System

Several databases in the LEXIS/NEXIS system provide useful legislative information. Information on the status of federal bills, bills from all 50 states, and "slip law" information for all the states can be retrieved from this system. The full text of Congressional bills and bills from California, Colorado, Massachusetts, Michigan, New Jersey, Ohio, and Pennsylvania are also available, in addition to such data as vote counts, topical legislative histories, committee reports, and public laws. Searchers who have access to this legislative information in the system also have access to the entire universe of legal and news information accessible in the system.

LEGAL SERVICES

The two most noted legal information systems are West Publishing Company's WESTLAW service and Mead Data Central's LEXIS service. Both provide users with instant electronic access to vast amounts of full-text legal information. The types of information included cover a wide range of types of materials as well as levels of government. The systems include the full text of bills and federal and state statutes. They also include the text of decisions from courts at various levels, from the U.S Supreme Court and U.S. Court of Appeals, to district and state courts. Administrative decisions from executive branch agencies, such as the Securities and Exchange Commission and National Labor Relations Board, are also available in these systems, as well as various opinions like State Attorney Generals' opinions. Regulatory information is included as well. The full text of the *Code of Federal Regulations* and *Federal Register* are easily accessible in WESTLAW and LEXIS. Both systems also enable users to search for and retrieve articles from law reviews, bar association journals, and other legal periodicals.

PUBLIC POLICY DATABASES AND NETWORKS

Public policies affect a wide range of professions and topical areas. Because of their broad scope, public policy issues can be found in just about any subject database. A few databases, and one network, should be noted here because they either focus on public policy issues or contain a large number of entries pertaining to public policy.

NTIS Database

Searchers of the NTIS (National Technical Information Service) database will find records representing U.S. government-sponsored research reports and analyses that are available to the public. These reports are sponsored by government agencies such as the U.S. Department of Energy, U.S. Department of Commerce, U.S. Department of Transportation, the National Aeronautics and Space Administration, and many more. A variety of state and local reports are also included in the database. The database is updated biweekly.

PAIS Database

The PAIS International Database is the online equivalent of the printed *PAIS Bulletin* from 1976 to date and the *PAIS FOREIGN LANGUAGE INDEX*. Materials cited in this database include periodical articles, books, pamphlets, reports, and documents from all levels of government. The coverage of the database is international with the focus being on public policy. The public policy issues addressed range from taxation and banking to transportation and international trade. The database is updated monthly.

GPO Monthly Catalog

The electronic equivalent of the printed *Monthly Catalog of U.S. Government Publications*, this database contains records reflecting publications issued by the legislative branch of government as well as all federal agencies. Because of the wide range of issues addressed by the government, the materials cited in this database run the gamut from libraries to medicine.

LOGIN

LOGIN is an information network that provides subscribers access to electronic mail and conferencing, and databases of information. Targeted at local government professionals, LOGIN contains records of over 30,000 innovative programs or approaches to a variety of local government functions. In each of these records a contact person and phone number is provided. LOGIN subscribers can also find articles from *City and State*, *Governing*, *American City and County*, and other publications to help keep them abreast of current trends. Individuals responsible for monitoring federal legislation will also find the Federal Legislative Tracking Service useful.

One of LOGIN's strengths lies in its communications aspect. In addition to electronic mail capabilities, users can seek the assistance of other local government professionals by posting a request for information or assistance on the network's Quest-Response Service for response from other users. The requests and responses can be viewed by all network users, facilitating an ongoing exchange of information.

Users may also access the Mayor's Forum, provided jointly by LOGIN and the U.S. Conference of Mayors. Information in the forum includes reports on topics of municipal interest, profiles of cities, U.S. Conference of Mayors' analyses of federal bills, and news of other topics of current interest.

Chapter 6

Marketing of Services

In a decade of dwindling budgets, public service providers need to promote their services actively in order to ensure that funds necessary to continue the service are received. As a service provider, marketing of services is a crucial component of legislative reference service, and your clientele has the power to influence an increase or decrease in your annual budget. Therefore you must be able to think like a salesperson and be prepared to sell the usefulness and necessity of your service to your primary clientele.

Correctly answering questions in a timely fashion and having brochures on available services are good for public relations, but they fail to alert non-users to what might be expected. Your service needs to be visible and easily accessible at all times to patrons. You need to actively seek out and alert new users to the wonderful information they can obtain from you. Because of the constant turnover in elected positions, it is essential to establish an ongoing active program to promote your service.

This program can consist of one or several different components, such as issuing newsletters, making presentations before target groups, and maintaining satellite reference desks. Described below are various activities that can be incorporated into an active marketing program.

ORIENTATIONS

Orientations to your reference service and its resources promote use of the service while assisting clients to use it effectively. These orientations should be presented not only at the start of new legislative sessions, but also, to take account of staff turnover, at regularly scheduled intervals throughout the year. All legislative staff from permanent consultants to part-time interns should be encouraged to attend.

Because orientation session attendees could include both constant researchers and infrequent users of the service, the orientation needs to provide a good overview of available services. The orientation should cover the services offered to legislative members and staff (including interlibrary loan and online search services), an overview of the resources available in the library, procedures for requesting information or materials, and options for delivery of those materials to the patron. An introduction to the use of the library's catalogs should be included as well as a tour of the library's public service areas and open stacks. And to encourage immediate use of the service, library cards (if applicable) and directory lists of key legislative reference staff should be issued at the end of the orientation session.

By providing orientation sessions you are promoting your service, and at the same time helping your patrons to utilize to good effect your service and your staff's time. The time devoted to presenting the orientations is more than gained back by your patrons' efficient use of the service.

SEMINARS

Seminars, a natural extension of orientation sessions, can garner even greater visibility for the legislative reference service. Conducting seminars on library research can be beneficial for patrons as well as for reference staff members involved in developing and presenting the seminars. It gives staff the opportunity to refresh their knowledge of the research process and the library's collections while providing them visibility within their government structure.

If desired, the reference service can also take on the role of seminar sponsor by arranging for the facilities, speakers, and appropriate publicity. This in turn allows an opportunity to alert seminar attendees to relevant resources on the seminar topic available from your library, and how your service can assist them in furthering research on the topic.

The New York State Library, for example, utilizes seminars as part of its outreach program. This library has sponsored seminars focusing on topics such as the state budget process and state administrative rule making, and has arranged for the appearance of suitable speakers from the academic community, state government, and the state library.

LETTERS

The first step in promoting your service is establishing initial contact with your patrons. This can be done by sending out personalized letters to elected and appointed officials and other members of your clientele at the start of each legislative session that either introduce them to or remind them of the reference services available to them. The letters should highlight any new services or changes, and they might be accompanied by a brochure describing available services, flyers on new publications, and an invitation to a personalized tour or orientation. For letters to committees or task forces you may also want to include a selective list of newly acquired titles of potential interest. Ideally, the letters should be from the state librarian, city librarian, or director of the reference service.

VISIBILITY AND PERSONAL CONTACT

It is desirable to establish personal contact with each of the officials served. However, for any one state legislature or other large governing body, this will not happen without considerable effort. Although you may meet some officials through the course of your work, you should strive to meet as many as them as possible. This is most easily achieved by attending city council and other government meetings. Attendance at these meetings has several advantages. First, it gives you visibility both personally and as a representative of the library. You will have the opportunity to voice your concerns regarding issues potentially affecting the library. Second, you will have a firsthand opportunity to observe and learn more about the legislative process and the people who shape the process. And third, you stay abreast of issues of current concern. This knowledge will enable you to prepare packets of information on the issues to be distributed to target patrons and other interested parties. Rather than waiting for people to contact you for the information, take the opportunity to alert them to its availability and thereby demonstrate your service is ready to meet their information needs in a timely manner.

You should also try to obtain appointments with key officials to discuss your concerns about the library or to report on its activities. These meetings can also be used to seek input on their information needs, and, if feasible, should occur on a regular basis.

USER-NEEDS ASSESSMENTS

One way of acquainting patrons with your service and your desire to serve them is to conduct a user-needs survey. This activity provides another opportunity to schedule appointments with elected officials and other members of your clientele. When conducting the survey, you will have the opportunity to discuss your services with selective clients while gathering valuable input on their information needs. Seek out potential suggestions for improvement of your services, and do not hesitate to express your appreciation for the time and input given by the patron. Be sure also to send participants a copy of any final document arising from the needs assessment survey.

SATELLITE SERVICE DESKS

Since legislators and government officials often have hectic work schedules, they are more apt to use those services that are convenient to use. Consider maintaining a satellite service desk in or near city hall, the state capitol, or wherever most of your clients work. A satellite desk requires only minimal staffing.

The function of a satellite desk is to facilitate requests for information, to explain services provided, and to provide a delivery point for information and materials requested. The service desk should be staffed by seasoned professionals who are knowledgeable of the library's collections and services and who will represent the library in a positive and efficient manner. Only the highest level of service should be provided at the satellite desk if the clientele is to realize the value and indispensable nature of your services.

Depending upon the size of the service area and the resources available, additional resources and services might be provided. If space permits, frequently used resources such as municipal or state codes, reports, and newspapers can be housed there. If staffing permits, materials and information requested at the satellite service desk can be delivered to the patrons' offices at scheduled times throughout the day. And if equipment is available, staff at the satellite desk can access selective online databases as needed. The satellite desk can indeed offer all the services offered by the main legislative reference desk.

The California State Library, for example, operates a satellite service desk in the state capitol building. Dubbed the "Capitol Branch," the satellite office occupies a small space on the second floor of the capitol building amidst Senate and Assembly offices. The room contains the California codes, the *California Code of Regulations*, legislative histories for the most recent five years, the local paper, three shelves of ready-reference materials, a computer workstation equipped to perform online database searches as appropriate, and a book return box. The service desk is staffed by only one librarian at a time, although three librarians are rotated through the branch at two-hour intervals. The librarians take requests for information or materials from legislative staff in person, by phone, or by mail. Books and other materials requested by patrons are delivered to the branch twice a day. The branch is heavily used by legislative staff and its use is steadily increasing. Users of the branch are constantly expressing their pleasure in the services provided and in having the service located so close to their offices.

OPEN HOUSE

Hosting an open house can also draw patrons into the library or satellite service area. The benefits of holding an open house include the ability to meet patrons in a social setting and the opportunity to discuss and promote your services in a relaxed setting. The only drawback is that it can often be difficult to convince your patrons to attend an open house.

Never forget you are dealing with legislative and other officials and their staff. You are competing with numerous other people, organizations, and lobbyists vying for a piece of their time and attention. Many of these competitors are, or hire, full-time professionals to publicize and lobby for their causes. So when you prepare invitations or flyers for your open house, remember you are competing with others for your clients' attention. Your efforts should be innovative and unique, i.e., in the nature of a real attention-grabber.

CURRENT AWARENESS PUBLICATIONS

Another means for promoting your services is to issue a series of publications focusing on topics of current interest to your patrons. These current awareness publications can take the form of a summary report on a topic or background paper, or they may consist of selective lists or annotated bibliographies of pertinent materials available in your library. Each of the formats has its advantages. For example, by issuing summary or background reports you can alert your clients to current issues while demonstrating the knowledge and abilities of reference staff. The other option of issuing bibliographies on the subject encourages circulation of the materials cited. An order form can even be included at the end of the bibliography to make it easier for patrons to request the items desired. Or, background papers can be accompanied as warranted by annotated bibliographies.

Regardless of the format chosen, these publications can be issued at regular intervals, or as the issues become topics of discussion. For example, issuing current awareness publications on reapportionment after each census would be appropriate, as would publications on a topic to be discussed at an upcoming city council meeting or legislative session. These publications should be sent to all members of your target audience unless prevailing government restrictions prohibit the mailing of unsolicited publications.

NEWSLETTERS

Newsletters alert your patrons to new services, trends, materials, or events, while incidentally keeping your service in their minds. Newsletters traditionally focus on the library and library-related events, but they can also focus on matters of community, state, or federal concern.

As a reference librarian, you know what issues your patrons are seeking information on. Your ability to spot trends in their needs gives you a chance to present your patrons with the information before they actually request it. A newsletter is the vehicle that enables you to inform your clients of events and matters that are of concern to them. The newsletter can contain brief articles and suggestions for further readings. It can also be used to report findings from recent user needs assessments.

OTHER PUBLICATIONS

A number of other publications can convey facts about the library and its reference services. A brochure or handout describing your services is essential to your promotional efforts. Attractive bookmarks listing your hours are often favored by patrons, while flyers can announce special events as needed. And lists of new acquisitions alert your patrons to new materials of possible interest.

When preparing new acquisition lists, be careful not to make the fatal mistake of preparing lists arranged by main entry, author, or title. No one enjoys scanning a long list of entries in search of a few potentially interesting books. Your patrons are generally interested in materials in specific subject areas, and it will take you very little time to arrange the entries in your new acquisitions list by subject categories. So make the extra effort to prepare a list that will be convenient for your patrons to use.

DISPLAYS

If you have display cases or areas, you may present informative displays on your resources and services. Such displays supply your patrons with additional facts regarding the library while furnishing you with an additional opportunity for outreach. Because displays are a good means for disseminating information, their availability is of value to your patrons.

Legislative and elected officials frequently have information on programs or topics they would like disseminated. Many of them would enjoy having display space made available to them. By offering them a display area, you are providing them with an additional service at the same time as you are taking advantage of another way of attracting your clients into the library. If appropriate, you might also bring their attention to related materials on their topic that they may want to include in the display.

CONCLUSION

As you plan your marketing strategy, remember your efforts need to be ongoing. Your activities need to appeal to your clients. They need to demonstrate the value of your services while highlighting how you can provide needed information and how this can facilitate their work. Your efforts should keep your library and services visible and on the minds of your patrons.

Chapter 7

Special Concerns

Legislative libraries are special libraries, and as such they have special concerns. The nature of their clientele and the clientele's work dictate that these concerns include ethics, privacy and confidentiality, the librarian/client relationship, response time, and after-hours access.

To respond to patrons' requests in a timely manner is a goal achieved by most libraries. For the legislative library, the goal is to provide requested information within time frames set by the patrons themselves. These time frames can range from a week or more for long-term projects to minutes, while the patron waits on the telephone for the answer.

The ability to respond to requests for information on a rush basis is essential. The patrons' need to have certain information on an urgent basis is often very real. Legislative members and staff are constantly working under strict deadlines. When they request information from your service they are taking a leap of faith that they will receive the exact data requested precisely when it is needed. If you fail to deliver the information or products as requested and this failure causes the patron undue problems, it will be extremely difficult to convince the patron to entrust important work to your service in the future. The even greater danger is that given the constant changes in legislative committee members and chairpersons, that same patron may someday chair or be part of a committee examining your budget or function. And surely enough, he or she will no doubt remember the one time that requested information from your service was not received.

Equally important to maintaining the credibility and usefulness of your service is your effectiveness in keeping all requests for information confidential. You have to be constantly aware of the sensitive nature of the legislative environment. If a patron inadvertently overhears you or your staff conversing among yourselves about another client's request, that patron may be leery of requesting information for fear that requests may not remain private. Politics is often compared to a game, and rightly so. It is important that you never, through lack of carelessness or breach of confidentiality, give one player an unfair advantage over another. A seemingly harmless conversation regarding an information request can have negative ramifications if inadvertently overheard by one of your patrons. All requests must be kept strictly confidential and the privacy of the patron must be respected at all times.

Confidentiality, trust, and the ability to deliver needed information all contribute to the establishment of a positive professional relationship between legislative reference service staff and patrons. Good relations encourage patrons to use your service as needed. Although your clientele consists of government officials and staff, they are also people. As such, they will inevitably use those services with which they feel comfortable.

Another ingredient contributing to their comfort level is a familiar face. They would prefer to deal with one or two people on a regular basis rather than a large number of people on an infrequent basis. This provides library staff and clients a proper opportunity to understand the needs and abilities of one another. Eventually personal links will be established that will empower library staff with an understanding of each patron's role in the legislative process, his or her responsibilities, work style, and information needs. The patron on the other hand will gain a proper understanding of the services provided by the library and of the workload and abilities of staff.

Library hours and library access are another issue you need to address. Although your library may close at five or six o'clock, your patrons often work long into the evening and may need access to the collection hours after the library has closed. Some legislative libraries provide keys to regular patrons or selected individuals.

A major concern with providing after-hours access is security. The greater the number of people with after-hours access to your facility, the greater the security risk. The chances grow that a door may be inadvertently left unlocked. An assessment of the overall increase in risk would have to encompass a number of factors such as security devices in place for items such as computers, nonpublic areas that can be separately locked, and overall building security if the library is located within a structure such as the capitol building. A number of precautions must be taken to minimize the risk of theft, such as restricting keys to regular patrons with a known need for after-hours access, installation of doors that automatically lock upon closing the door, etc.

The positive effect of providing after-hours access, however, outweighs the concerns. You must remember that one of the prime functions of a library is to provide access to information. If your patrons find they are unable to get needed information because the library is often closed, they will regard its usefulness as limited. But if they have access to the library when they need it, they will find it an invaluable resource in fulfilling their needs. Supplying patrons with a key to the library also instills in them a sense that the library is truly their library.

Providing such access does not mean automatically passing out keys to all your patrons. You know your clientele. You know your frequent patrons and their needs. You know which ones truly do need access to the collection in the early morning or evening. You know which of your clients will both benefit and appreciate 24-hour access to the library.

You should have a written policy in place regarding hours of access. You should also have policies and procedures in place regarding the services that will or will not be provided. In most instances the policies and procedures can be applied in meeting the requests for information you receive. In some cases, however, the requests will fall into a nebulous category that invokes questions of ethics, no matter how detailed your service policy may be. For example, the policy can state that requests in support of personal campaigning will not be accepted. Yet undoubtedly you will occasionally find yourself in a situation such as the following. A patron, the chief of staff of a powerful legislator, telephones the library. The legislator for which the patron works is up for election and is running against Mr. XYZ. (Mr. XYZ is a former member of Congress who left office under unusual circumstances.) The patron requests photocopies of all pages in the Congressional Record in which Mr. XYZ's name appears. You inform your patron regarding your policy against accepting requests pertaining to personal campaigning. The patron tells you the information sought is not campaign-related and insists you accept the request. This places you in the awkward position of sensing that the request *is* campaign-related, but you cannot very well tell the patron you suspect he or she is not being truthful. Unfortunately, there is no standard procedure for handling situations such as these. Circumstances, relationships, politics, and numerous other factors vary from case to case. In this situation, because the request entails considerable work on the part of library staff, the librarian may be able to negotiate the date range or amount of material to be obtained. Another option is to have library staff mark or paperclip the appropriate pages in the Congressional Record to be copied and make a photocopy machine available to the requestor so that he or she can do the actual copying. These options help reduce the amount of work performed by library staff, but still do not address the issue of whether or not the request actually is campaign-related. Unfortunately, you may never really ascertain that information.

Chapter 8

Conclusion

The roles and responsibilities of a legislative reference librarian are not to be taken lightly. Misinformation or lack of adequate information can potentially lead to poor legislation that can negatively impact hundreds of people, while provision of accurate and appropriate information can assist lawmakers in drafting legislation that benefits society at large. Nowhere else is the impact of a reference librarian's work more evident than it is in the legislative process.

The legislative reference librarian also has the ability to provide legislators with either a positive or negative impression of the role of libraries and librarians in their jurisdictions. In these times of tight financial constraints and downsizing, libraries and librarians must demonstrate their value to society if they wish to remain competitive in the budget process. Libraries are physical facilities where materials and information are stored. It is the librarians who transform these facilities into libraries as we know them, and it is the librarians who ultimately determine the future libraries will experience.

Appendix A

Contact Information for Associations

Council of State Governments
P.O. Box 11910
Iron Works Pike
Lexington, KY 40578-1910
(606) 231-1939

ICMA
777 North Capitol St., NE
Ste. 500
Washington, DC 20002-4201
(202) 962-3680

National Association
of Counties
440 First St., NW
Washington, DC 20001
(202) 393-6226

National Association of Towns
and Townships
1522 K St., NW
Ste. 730
Washington, DC 20005
(202) 737-5200

National Conference
of State Legislatures
1560 Broadway
Ste. 700
Denver, CO 80202-5140
(303) 830-2200

National Governor's Association
Hall of the States
444 North Capitol St.,
Ste. 250
Washington, DC 20001-1572
(202) 624-5300

National League of Cities
1301 Pennsylvania Ave., NW
Washington, DC 20004
(202) 626-3000

Appendix B

Contact Information for Online Services and Databases

ISIS
Council of State Governments
P.O. Box 11910
Iron Works Pike
Lexington, KY 40578-1910
(606) 231-1939

LEGISNET
National Conference of State
  Legislatures
1560 Broadway
Ste. 700
Denver, CO 80202-5140

LEGISLATE
111 Massachusetts Ave., NW
Washington, DC 20001
(202) 898-2300

Legi-Tech Corp.
1029 J St.
Ste. 450
Sacramento, CA 95814
(916) 447-1886

LEXIS/NEXIS
Mead Data Central
9443 Springboro Pike
P.O. Box 933
Dayton, OH 45401
(800) 543-6862

LOCIS
Library of Congress
Washington, DC 20559
(202) 707-2905

LOGIN
LOGIN Information Services
245 East 6th St.
Ste. 809
St. Paul, MN 55101
(800) 328-1921

National Technical Information
  Service
Office of Product Management
F300
5285 Port Royal Rd.
Springfield, VA 22161
(703) 487-4929

Public Affairs Information
  Service Inc.
521 West 43rd St.
New York, NY 10036-4396
(212) 736-6629

STATENET, a service of
  Information for Public
  Affairs
1900 14th St.
Sacramento, CA 95814
(916) 444-0840

WESTLAW
West Publishing Company
50 W. Kellog Blvd.
P.O. Box 64526
St. Paul, MN 55164-0526
(800) 328-9352

Appendix C

State Legislative Reference Bureaus

Alabama State Legislative
    Reference Service
613 State House Montgomery,
AL 36130
(205) 242-7560

Alaska Legislative Reference
Library
State Capitol
Juneau, AK 99811
(907) 465-3808

Arizona Department
    of Library, Archives
    and Public Records
1700 West Washington
Phoenix, AZ 85007
(602) 542-3701

Arkansas State Bureau
    of Legislative Research
State Capitol, Room 315
Little Rock, AR 72201
(510) 682-1937

California State Library
Capitol Branch
State Capitol, Room 2019
Sacramento, CA 95814
(916) 445-3551

Colorado State Legislative
    Council
State Capitol
Denver, CO 80203
(303) 866-4799

Congressional Research
    Service
Library of Congress
Washington, DC 20540
(202) 707-8997

Connecticut State Legislative
    Library
Legislative Office Building
Room 5400
Hartford, CT 06106
(203) 240-8888

Delaware Legislative Council
Legislative Hall
Dover, DE 19901
(302) 739-5808

Florida State Division
    of Legislative Library
    Services
701 Capitol
Tallahassee, FL 32399-1400
(904) 488-2812

Georgia House Research Office
Legislative Office Building 18
Capitol Square
Atlanta, GA 30334
(404) 656-3206

Georgia Senate Research Office
Legislative Office Building
18 Capitol Square
Atlanta, GA 30334
(404) 656-0015

Hawaii State Legislative
    Reference Bureau
1177 Alakea St.
Honolulu, HI 96813
(808) 587-0690

Idaho State Library
325 West State St.
Boise, ID 83702
(208) 334-2150

Illinois State Legislative
    Reference Bureau
112 State Capitol
Springfield, IL 62706
(212) 782-6625

Indiana Legislative Information
    Center
302 State House
Indianapolis, IN 46204
(317) 232-9856

Iowa State Legislative Service
    Bureau
State House
Des Moines, IA 50319
(515) 281-3312

Kansas State Library
Statehouse
Topeka, KS 66612
(913) 296-3296

Kentucky State Legislative
    Research Commission
State Capitol
Frankfort, KY 40601
(502) 564-8100

Louisiana State Legislative
    Reference Library
P.O. Box 94012
Baton Rouge, LA 70804-9012
(504) 342-2431

Maine State Law
and Legislative Reference
Library
State House
Augusta, ME 04333
(207) 287-1600

Maryland Department
of Legislative Reference
90 State Circle
Annapolis, MD 21401
(410) 841-3810

Massachusetts State Library
State House
Boston, MA 02133
(617) 727-2590

Michigan State Legislative
Services Bureau
P.O. Box 30036
Lansing, MI 48909-7536
(517) 373-0472

Minnesota Legislative
Reference Library
645 State Office Building
St. Paul, MN 55155
(612) 296-8338

Mississippi State Legislative
Reference Bureau
P.O. Box 1018
Jackson, MS 39215-1018
(601) 359-3135

Missouri State Legislative
Library
State Capitol
Jefferson City, MO 65101
(314) 751-4633

Montana State Library
1515 East 6th Ave.
Helena, MT 59620
(406) 444-3004

Nebraska State Legislative
Reference Library
State Capitol
Lincoln, NE 68509
(402) 471-0075

Nevada State Library
and Archives
Capitol Complex
Carson City, NV 89710
(702) 687-5160

New Hampshire State Library
20 Park St.
Concord, NH 03301
(603) 271-2239

New Jersey State Office
of Legislative Services
Library
Trenton, NJ 08625-0068
(609) 984-4321

New Mexico Legislative
Counsel Service
State Capitol
Santa Fe, NM 87503
(505) 986-4600

New York Legislative Library
337 State Capitol
Albany, NY 12224
(518) 455-4000

State of North Carolina
   Legislative Library
Legislative Office Building
Raleigh, NC 27603
(919) 733-9390

North Dakota State Library
604 East Blvd.
Bismarck, ND 58505-0800
(701) 224-4662

Ohio Legislative Service
   Commission
77 South High St.
Columbus, OH 43266-0342
(614) 446-7434

Oklahoma State Legislative
   Reference Division
Department of Libraries
200 NE 18th St.
Oklahoma City, OK 73105
(405) 521-2502

Oregon State Legislative
   Library
State Capitol
Salem, OR 97310
(503) 378-8871

Pennsylvania Legislative
   Reference Bureau
Main Capitol Building
Harrisburg, PA 17120-0033
(717) 787-4816

Rhode Island State Library
State House
Providence, RI 02903-1120
(401) 277-2473

South Carolina Legislative
   Counsel
State House
Columbia, SC 29211
(803) 734-2413

South Dakota Legislative
   Research
State Capitol
Pierre, SD 57501-5070
(605) 773-4498

Tennessee Office of Legal
   Services
War Memorial Building
Nashville, TN 37219
(615) 741-3091

Texas State Library
Legislative Reference Library
Capitol Station
Austin, TX 78711
(512) 463-1252

Utah Office of Legislative
  Research and General
  Counsel
State Capitol
Salt Lake City, UT 84114
(801) 538-1032

Vermont Department
  of Libraries
Reference and Law Division
Montpelier, VT 05602
(802) 828-3268

Virginia Division
  of Legislative Services
Legislative Reference Library
910 Capitol St.
Richmond, VA 23219
(804) 786-3591

Washington State Library
P.O. Box 42478
Olympia, WA 98504-2478
(206) 753-4027

West Virginia Legislative
  Reference Library
State Capitol
Charleston, WV 25305
(304) 558-2153

Wisconsin State Legislative
  Reference Bureau
100 North Hamilton St.
Madison, WI 53701-2037
(608) 266-0344

Wyoming State Library
Legislative Service Office
State Capitol
Cheyenne, WY 82002
(307) 777-7881

Appendix D

Sample Letter to Legislators
(printed on Legislative Reference Bureau Letterhead)

September 1, 1998

Honorable John Doe
State House, Room 222
Capitol, OZ 94523

Dear Representative Doe:

Congratulations on your recent election to the State House of Representatives. As the new session begins, please let me alert you to the legislative reference services available to you and your staff from the library's Legislative Reference Bureau located in Room 89 of the State House. Staffed by experienced legislative librarians, the Legislative Reference Bureau is prepared to meet all your information needs.

The Reference Bureau provides access to both state and out-of-state legal materials, government publications, newspapers from across the state, magazines and journals, and other materials covering a full spectrum of topics. Staff of the Bureau can answer your reference questions, access hundreds of electronic databases to locate information, deliver the materials requested, provide background information for potential legislation, assist in answering constituent questions, provide 50-state legislative surveys, and purchase materials upon request. Please do not hesitate to call upon the Reference Bureau to assist you with these or other information needs.

The Bureau also compiles biweekly publications in the fields of Law and Government, Health and Human Services, Natural Resources and the Environment, and Technology, which highlight new publications of interest in these areas. Sample copies are enclosed.

Although you and your staff have extremely busy schedules, I encourage you and your staff to attend one of the upcoming orientations to the use of the Legislative Reference Bureau scheduled for Tuesday, September 9th from 8:30-9:00 a.m., Wednesday September 10th from 5:00-6:00 p.m., or Friday, September 12th from noon to 1:00 p.m.

In the meantime, please do not hesitate to call upon the Legislative Reference Bureau at 553-5786 to assist you with your information needs.

Sincerely,

George Smith
Director, Legislative Reference Bureau

encs.

Appendix E

Sample Letter to New Committee Chairpersons
(on Legislative Reference Service Letterhead)

January 3, 1998

Senator Doe
Chairperson, Senate Education Committee
State Capitol, Room 1443
Reno, NV 98765

Dear Senator Doe:

As the new session begins, I would like to take this opportunity to alert you and your committee staff to the services available to you from the Legislative Reference Bureau in Room 292 of the capitol building. Professional staff on duty in the Bureau from 9:00 a.m. - 6:00 p.m. can answer your reference questions, respond to your information requests, electronically access hundreds of databases, and locate and provide you with materials ranging from copies of bills to major newspapers from across the nation. Requests can be submitted to the bureau by phone, by mail, by telefacsimile, or in person.

The Bureau also issues *Trends in Education*, a biweekly annotated list of new publications dealing with education and education-related topics. Sample issues are enclosed for your perusal. Your name has been added to the distribution list for this publication.

Please contact the Bureau with the names of any staff persons whom you would also like to add to the distribution list for this publication.

We will also be offering orientations on use of the Bureau during the week of January 20th. The exact dates and times are enclosed. I realize you have a busy schedule, but if you have time, please contact the bureau and we can arrange a quick orientation to fit your time schedule.

If you have any questions about the Bureau and its services, or have a request for information, please do not hesitate to contact me at 444-5151.

Sincerely,

Albert Smith
Director, Legislative Reference Bureau

encs.

Appendix F

Sample Current Awareness Publication
(issued on Legislative Reference Service Letterhead)

ENVIRONMENTAL PUBLICATIONS IN THE NEWS

Issue # 47   September 15, 1998

The items cited herein represent recent publications pertaining to environmental issues on a state and national basis. Copies of the items cited can be requested from the library in person by stopping by Room 425 in the Statehouse, by telephone (823-4476), or via electronic mail (@SHLIBRARY). To facilitate your order, please request items by request number.

Biweekly lists of new publications in the areas of energy, health and human services, education, law and law enforcement, technology, and government are also available. If you wish to be added to the distribution list for any of the above, please contact the Legislative Reference Service.

Air Pollution

The Cost of Clean Air. Prepared for the Council for Environmental Balance. (National Clean Air Research Associates, Angwin, CA) August 21, 1998, 57 p.
> "This study provides a detailed cost analysis of the factors involved in cleaning up the air in the South Coast Basin area."
> (Request # 98-427)

Federal Bill to Reform Air Pollution Standards. (The Legislative Journal, Fairbanks, AK) August 1998, p. 74-77.

The article examines S42, which seeks to impose new air pollution standards, establish new methods of measuring air pollution levels, and gives states a new role in enforcement of the standards.

(Request # 98-428)

Rice Field Burning: Long-Term Effects on the Environment. (The Daily News, Vacaville, CA) August 14, 1998, p. B3.

A synopsis of recent studies on the long-term environmental impact of burning rice fields is presented in this article.

(Request # 98-429)

Appendix G

Sample Topical Awareness Publication

No. 34   March 1993

DOWNSIZING

Given the present economy, most employers are downsizing their organizations. The materials cited below address various aspects of downsizing, from tips on how to downsize, to the anxiety and stress faced by the employees who have been displaced, to those who survived the layoff process. These materials are just a few of the more recent items on the topic available from the Legislative Reference Service.

1. "Downsizing and Worker Assistance: The Latest Survey Results," by John Holbrook and Eric Spiner. In: *Employment Trends*, vol. 3, no. 14 (February 1993) p. 57-74. The survey shows that two-thirds of all responding organizations had downsized over the past year and that 13% of them already anticipate further downsizing in the upcoming year.

2. "Help in Making Tough Layoff Decisions," by Jamie Kates, Leslie Femer, and George Stein. In: *Corporate Conscience*, vol. 52, no. 12 (December 1992) p. 3-11. The article points out that, in general, front line supervisors are given the task of deciding which workers should be laid off. There is, however, a fairer method of deciding who goes and who stays. This method also removes much of the stress from those supervisors charged with selecting those individuals to be cut from the workforce.

3. "How Workers React to Co-Worker Layoffs," by Ron Bueler. In: *Journal of Work and Psychology*, vol. 1, no. 1 (January 1993)

p. 47-49+. The results of a study on the effect of co-worker layoffs on remaining employees were examined at 15 organizations of various sizes, industries, and locations. In general, those employees that survived the layoff process were found to be less content with their jobs, more withdrawn from the organization, and discontent with management.

4. *What to Do When You Lose Your Job*, by Susan Katz. (Whitick, CA, Prattle Publishing Co.) 1993. 147 p.

(Sample back page to the topical publication.)

OBTAINING THE PUBLICATIONS CITED
Please fill out the order form below. Please note that all requests should include the list number and item number.

DISTRIBUTION LIST
If you wish to be placed on the mailing list for this publication, call us at 987-2345, or send your request to:

Legislative Reference Bureau
Capitol, Room 423
Linzer, CO 98608

ORDER FORM
Please send the following publications from Issue # 4, March 1993:

Item

Number(s)_____

Name: _____

(House/Senate) Office:_____

Room Number:_____

Appendix H

Sample Cover Sheet for a Printout Resulting from an Online Database Search

LEGISLATIVE REFERENCE BUREAU
555-1234

THIS PACKET OF INFORMATION IS FOR:

NAME_____

(SENATE/HOUSE) OFFICE_____

STATE HOUSE ROOM NUMBER_____

Enclosed is a computer printout of information you requested on the topic of_____.

The following databases were searched in response to your request:

_____

_____

_____

_____

If the attached printout contains citations, the items cited can be retrieved for you by library staff. If you desire to have library staff retrieve the items for you, please complete and return the attached form with your printout.

If you have any questions regarding this information, please contact:

_____

Telephone Number 555-0909

Appendix I

Sample Request Form
for Retrieval of Documents

TO: Legislative Reference Bureau
        State House, Room 222

REQUEST FOR RETRIEVAL OF MATERIALS

DATE OF REQUEST:_____

NAME_____

(ASSEMBLY/SENATE) OFFICE_____

BUILDING/ROOM NUMBER_____

TELEPHONE NUMBER_____

Please retrieve and deliver the items highlighted or checked on the attached list.

Date by which the items are needed_____

When the materials have been gathered:

__ Call me, or _____ for pick up

__ Send the materials to my office via

    __ Messenger

    __ Regular delivery service

    __ And call to alert me to the fact they are being sent

Appendix J

Sample Newsletter

January 24, 1998

INFORMATION BITS

News from the Legislative Reference Bureau

*Orientations to Use
of Legislative Reference
Bureau Scheduled*

Four one-hour orientations to the Legislative Reference Bureau have been scheduled from noon to 1:00 p.m., February 1-4, 1998. The orientation sessions will acquaint you with the services available to you, plus provide you with guidelines on how to use the service in the most effective manner. Following the orientation, an optional tour of the library will be conducted from 1:00 - 2:00 p.m. To sign up for an orientation session, call 555-5523 or stop by the Bureau in Room 222.

*Reference Bureau Welcomes
Sally Smith*

Sally Smith joined the staff of the Legislative Reference Bureau on August 1st as a Reference Specialist. Sally's area of expertise is environmental issues. She holds a Masters of Library Science degree from Claremont College and a Master of Science degree in Biology from Simmons College. Prior to working for the Reference Bureau she served as an Air Pollution Analyst with the E.P.A., as the Legislative Policy Analyst for the State Farmers' Association, and as the Science Reference Librarian at the University of Texas. Sally can be reached at 555-5546. Welcome aboard, Sally!

Three New NCSL Videotapes Acquired

Three new videotapes just released by the National Conference of State Governments have been acquired. The topics of the tapes are: Long-Term Environmental Impact of Disposable Diapers in Landfills, Innovative Programs in Reducing Child Abuse, and The Use of Technology in Tracking Convicted Drug Dealers. The videos can be viewed in the Reference Bureau A/V room, or can be borrowed for one week.

District Maps Accessible on Legislative Information System

State district maps can now be viewed in the Legislative Information System. To access the file, type: ACCESSLIBMAPS. The system will then present you with a menu of the districts or areas you wish to view. Paper copies of the maps are also available at the Legislative Reference Bureau.

New Studies on the Los Angeles Riots Available

The library has just acquired two new studies by the Non-Profit Center on the Elimination of Violence that focus on the causes for the 1992 riots in Los Angeles. The first study examines the socio-economic conditions of the Black Community and Asian American Communities in South Central Los Angeles six months prior to the riot. The second study analyzes the changing condition of race relations in the area from 1990 to the time of the riots.

Index